"When Dave Harris spins a yarn there is no need for Paul Harvey to show up for the rest of the story. His riveting vignettes in Treasure Trove in Passing Vessels end with the same punch with which they start. This talented storyteller weaves true-life memories on the loom of well-chosen words. The result is a heartwarming read that has both the gentle feel of a cardigan-clad Fred Rogers and the tongue-in-cheek wit of Garrison Keillor. Much like his grandfather, Milton Richards (AKA Milo Oblinger) who wrote the popular Dick Kent book series in the 1920s, what Dave Harris writes is bound to be read."

—Greg Asimakoupoulos, pastor, author and poet, Naperville, IL

Bruce & Ella,

It was *you* who attracted us to the "treasured" Olympians! I've thoroughly enjoyed your hospitality and warm welcome.

God bless,

Dave Harris

12/2004

360-779-3837

Treasure Trove in Passing Vessels

Treasure Trove in Passing Vessels

Ordinary people leading intriguing lives

Dave Harris

iUniverse, Inc.
New York Lincoln Shanghai

Treasure Trove in Passing Vessels
Ordinary people leading intriguing lives

iUniverse, Inc.

For information address:
iUniverse, Inc.
2021 Pine Lake Road, Suite 100
Lincoln, NE 68512
www.iuniverse.com

ISBN: 0-595-31311-6

To my six treasured, witty, loving and articulate granddaughters who make me of all men most richly blessed: Emma Walker, Brenna Everingham, Austin Everingham, Kristen Wagner, Ashley Wagner and Jennifer Wagner. I look forward to writing more about your wise sound bites and adventures in future stories. I love you.

Wonder is that possession of the mind that enchants the emotions while never surrendering reason. It is a grasp on reality that does not need constant high points in order to be maintained, nor is it made vulnerable by the low points of life's struggle. It sees in the ordinary the extraordinary, and finds in the extraordinary the re-affirmations for what it already knows. Wonder blasts the soul, that is the spiritual and the skeleton, the body, the material. Wonder interprets life through the eyes of eternity while enjoying the moment, but never lets the moment's revision exhaust the eternal. Wonder makes life's enchantment real and knows when and where enchantment must lie. Wonder knows how to read the shadows because it knows the nature of light. Wonder knows that while you cannot look at the light, you cannot look at anything else without it. It is not exhausted by childhood, but finds its key there. It is a journey like a walk through the woods over the usual obstacles and around the common distractions while the voice of direction leads saying this is the way, walk ye in it. Ravi Zacharias

Contents

Foreword

Why did I write this book?

Listening to the conversations of talk shows, carpools and office chatter for some 37 years, I came to understand that relatively few people focused on a larger world of beauty, peace and joy that my family and close friends have known for years. I observed that most folks compartmentalize their lives. Work was what they did from 7:30 to 4:00. If they worship, they do that for an hour Sunday morning. Family got undivided attention when it was time to open another compartment of their lives.

My co-workers would wonder why I came up online over a work issue on my day off. I fought the compartmentalization I saw others practicing. I wanted work to be productive, fun, relaxing, social and spiritual within reason and limits imposed by the powers that be, both externally and within myself. Times with family, friends, vanpool, church or community were to be no different. They all blended together. I learned that life cannot be compartmentalized—not even major milestones and passages. It's not a matter of going from conception to birth to childhood to adulthood to death to eternity. My eternity has begun. I expect to be doing things 500 years from now that are not all that different than what I'm doing today or preparing myself to do. I am not so much looking forward to a future heaven as much as I participate today in the kingdom of the heavens, right now. A song by Phil McHugh says, *I wanna get so close to Him that it's no big change on that day that Jesus calls my name!* Dallas Willard wrote *Divine Conspiracy*, a book that impacted me as few others. Let's not prepare for death. Let's prepare for life—abundant, busy, endless life.

If you could only read one book—mine or Willard's—toss mine as far as you possibly can, stop what you're doing and get his book today—now.

Call it a worldview—a spectacular one, not in any way limited to me, but shared by many. Here's but a glimpse, as described in *Divine Conspiracy*:

> While I was teaching in South Africa…Matthew Dickason took me out to see the beaches near his home in Port Elizabeth….I stood in stunned silence and then slowly walked toward the waves. Words cannot capture the view that confronted me. I saw space and light and texture and color and power…that

seemed hardly of this earth....God sees this all the time....Great tidal waves of joy must constantly wash through his being....We pay a lot of money to get a tank with a few tropical fish in it and never tire of looking at their brilliant iridescence and marvelous forms and movements. But God has seas full of them, which he constantly enjoys....Human beings can lose themselves in card games or electric trains and think they are fortunate. But to God there is available, "towering clouds of gases trillions of miles high, backlit by nuclear fires in newly forming stars, galaxies cartwheeling into collision and sending explosive shock waves boiling through millions of light-years of time and space." These things are all before him, along with numberless unfolding rosebuds, souls, and songs—and immeasurably more of which we know nothing.

If we would but open our eyes, we can see such marvels in you. People fascinate me. Just one of the cells in your body is so complex that the previous paragraph can scarcely describe what's going on it that cell—in you. And then, there are the ingenious constructs of your eyes and ears and heart. *Such knowledge is too wonderful for me, too lofty for me to attain* (Psalm 139, NIV).

Over 37 years, it has been my privilege to get *paid* for writing stories about people—ordinary folks who became treasured people. I have often said that there are 10 stories inside anyone—you. This book, with fresh portrayals of lifelong observations, will illustrate how ordinary individuals are treasures of insight, wisdom and created beauty, the everyday experiences of common folk like you and me—the joys I've had sharing with many of you over nearly 60 years. These are but samples. If you don't find yourself included here, perhaps you will be in a sequel.

I hope this book will prompt us all to see the marvels within the souls of our sons, daughters, siblings, parents, co-workers, pals and neighbors, and be so awed by what we see that we quicken our steps to close the gap between ourselves and their Creator who longs to have daily intimate conversations with us.

Dave Harris
Poulsbo, Washington
February 14, 2004

Secret Ambassador's Levers

Edith Brown had that soft, wet gaze that peeked deep into your soul. She had frizzy gray hair and plain glasses, but that special, far-away look in her eye and her glorious smile revealed an astonishing inner beauty.

I experienced her healing touch but once. If you were particularly "fortunate," she would explain how the nerves in your foot affected other parts of your body, and she would massage your feet to prove her point.

One Christmas season I worked for the Post Office to help with their busiest time of the year. My route included the home of Edith and Jimmy Brown. Sorted mail would wait for my arrival in a locked box in the neighborhood. Usually a handful of letters and Christmas cards lasted completely down one side of the block and back. Then I'd grab another handful. That big stack didn't last the whole block where Edith lived. Each day, I'd leave a bulging four-inch pile of personal mail at her house. She and Jimmy got more cards than anybody else I've ever known.

I've noticed over the years that people with certain breathtaking gifts come to earth on loan for only a short time. God longs for their company and, sad for us, they spare no time in complying with the summons. Edith was one of those on God's short leash. She came down with cancer. I would say "unfortunately," but how do I know that? Too often I've seen beauty and strength emerge from suffering, and "unfortunately" comes from a limited mind like mine.

As it frequently happens, Edith was one who had much to teach us before she departed. She had given Mom a simple plant well before she died. Mom took that little thing home, nurtured it, watered it…but nothing happened. It just "sat in its squat," as Zig Ziglar would say.

When Edith died, friends and family arranged a simple memorial service at Interbay Covenant Church. But who were all the many strangers? The endless line of people coming in packed the place. Who would have expected such an overflow crowd to remember the plain and quiet Edith Brown?

Many strangers got up to pay tribute to Edith. People loved her for what she did for them. Edith, we discovered, was a secret ambassador. Her admirers, often needy, told of how she quietly brought them food, clothing or blankets. She told

1

no one. None of us knew. Not even Jimmy knew all that she was up to. And she profoundly touched the lives of unknown hundreds.

After Edith's burial, it happened. That do-nothing plant that Edith gave to Mom perked up. Somehow, it knew what happened to Edith. Jimmy virtually climbed the walls after Edith died. The plant, however, actually did. It sent vines, full of life, all over the room.

Going to heaven isn't just sitting on a cloud and playing a harp. We will be working hard on a God-given assignment. Scripture says we will reign with Christ. Dallas Willard suggests we start getting our act together now so we can effectively carry out our assignments when we step over on the other side.

I think Edith is busier than most in heaven. To start, she explored celestial mechanical rooms until she found a row of levers. "I wonder what would happen if I move these forward...oops!"

An angel, Buzz, spotted her. "Careful with those, Edith! Shove those levers too far, and you might overdo their function."

"What are they?"

"I'm not totally sure; we haven't used them much since Eden."

"What do they do, Buzz?"

"Oh, they are some kind of earth-plant growth accelerators."

Heaven, This Bud's for You

No one ever had a more suitable baseball name than Homer Cummings. He looked like a lovable cartoon character. This retired truck driver's ear twisted up like a wrestler's cauliflower. Everyone called him Bud, and I think he had gone a few rounds in the ring in his day as a boxer. God pretty much left Bud's classic outward appearance the same. I think He was amused at the sight—stubby, muscular, a bit of a potbelly, rickety arthritic legs, pug nose, beady eyes and a permanent-but-fun-loving scowl. The outside was rough, but somewhere God got hold of his heart and reshaped it, giving it the unmistakable Master's Touch.

Bud loved softball and organized the church team as its take-charge, no-nonsense player-coach. In later years, the old legs stiffened, and so Bud limited his activity to setting up the field and coaching the younger players. Mess up, though, and Bud didn't mince words. The message was squeaky-clean, but pointed and direct. He softened them with a hand on your shoulder or a slap on the backside and a wink.

It was a half-hour before the game. The field was bare, and Bud tucked the bases under his arm. Dropping one at first, he shuffled over to line up second base. Looking to the ground, then slowly over to third, he gave the base a soft kick to move it 2 inches. He gazed straight down at the base by his feet. He just stood there. Then he crumpled to the ground. Out.

His funeral attracted teammates and opponents alike. Everyone knew he was already scribbling the celestial batting order. Once again he'd be lead-off hitter, knowing his heavenly mobility was to be greatly enhanced.

Pastor Tommy Paino led the team and the rather large cheering section in a memorial celebration. Team tears betrayed how much they missed him. But it was a time to rejoice, and yes, even sing.

Before the emotion-choked audience lifted their voices in a rendition of *Take Me Out to the Ball Game*, Tommy had outdone himself in his customary down-to-earth but eloquent tribute:

"...God tapped the Old Slugger on the shoulder and whispered in his ear. 'Son,' He beckoned. 'Slide on home.'"

But in keeping with his promise we are looking forward to a new heaven and a new earth, the home of righteousness. So then, dear friends, since you are looking forward to this, make every effort to be found spotless, blameless and at peace with him. 2 Peter 3:13-14 (NIV)

The Call—Wrong Number?

My family on Dad's side was big into nicknames. Sometimes the origin was a mystery. Uncle Merrill and Aunt Alberta were "Bump and Peaches." I have half of that figured out. I was more puzzled with the nicknames of Uncle Roy and Aunt Roberta—"Tim and Bobby." Go figure.

Roy and Merrill—"Tim" and "Bump"—became Methodist ministers, thanks to the evangelical fervor of Park Avenue Methodist Church in Minneapolis, and its heart for young people.

Roy's calling to the ministry had a rather inauspicious beginning. It was an intensely sacred time of testimony. One after another, a young man or woman in the youth group stood and told what the Lord was doing in his or her life. I recall many services like this. When I was a teenager, sometimes these testimony services took place at camp at a bonfire. The young person would grab a small stick, called a "fagot," and throw it into the fire to symbolize the surrender of oneself in consecration to God's service. For obvious reasons, such occasions these days are no longer called "fagot services."

But a generation ago, Uncle Roy, er, Tim, still in school, was in attendance at the testimony service. A large girl, he recalls, was brimming with emotion and commitment. She summoned the courage to stand. A hush fell over the crowd. Haltingly, she announced her calling.

"God...has called me...to serve Him...in the mission field...with...with... with Roy Harris!"

Having never dated or even barely spoken to the girl, Roy was floored as every eye in the room focused on him.

God had other ideas and another mate in mind.

"Dear friends, do not believe every spirit, but test the spirits to see whether they are from God" (1 John 4:1, NIV).

Dad's Fifty-Cent Chit

Dad got on that World War II train in Minneapolis and couldn't find a seat.

"I 'walked' all the way from California to Boston," he told us kids with a smile years later.

The Coast Guard had given him 50-cent chits to pay for his meals in the dining car. Though he seldom got to rest in the coach car, the steward finally seated him for lunch. Dad picked up a menu and swallowed hard. Two dollars would barely buy him the cheapest entrée listed. A 50-cent chit fell far short, and Dad didn't have any money to spare until he got to Boston and collected his pay. That would be three days away. Could he go on a fast that long?

Presently the waiter approached the young serviceman.

"What can I get for you, Sailor?"

Dad closed the menu.

"I guess nothing," he said quietly. "I don't have enough to cover it. If you could just bring me a glass of water."

Perhaps the waiter could see the disappointment on Dad's face. He put his hand on Dad's shoulder.

"You have a military meal chit? Let's see."

Dad pulled out his 50-cent coupon.

"Son, don't you know? That chit will buy you anything you want on the menu!"

It didn't end there. Three Coast Guard seamen had come aboard with little money and no chits.

With the waiter's blessing, all four ate on one 50-cent chit, three times a day.

Dad's story reminded me of a couple who gathered their life savings to buy passage aboard a vessel sailing from Europe to America. They would be a week or two at sea in a tiny lower-deck cabin and they had packed a flat box with bread and whatever provisions they didn't think would spoil.

After three days, having picked over meager morsels, the husband craved a hot drink.

"Honey, I'm going up on deck and buy a cup of coffee. I don't care what it costs."

Twenty minutes later he returned to the cabin with wide eyes.

"You won't believe it, Honey, but all the meals are free!"

Fix-It Man

Dad could fix anything—almost. If we brought him a broken electric train, watch, radio, TV or remote control car, Dad could diagnose it and repair it in a hurry.

When my brother Thom and I were little, Dad began a tradition of bringing home two or three ducklings for Easter. We kept them out in the garage under a warm light with a feeder and a drinking device where they could get water. They'd grow up fast, and we'd let them waddle around the yard. They were fast. Run as fast as I could, I never caught up with them. Dad could. Dad never ran. He just walked faster than anyone, and he could catch those ducks.

Don't get too attached to those ducks. Before the year was up, Dad would chop off their heads, and we'd have duck for dinner. Then, when Easter would roll around, we'd have three new, yellow, fuzzy baby ducks. We knew the routine. Fix up a box for them in the garage. Get out the lamp, the feeder and the water jar. We enjoyed picking up those cuddly babies and cradling one at a time in our cupped hands.

One day, Thom went out to the garage to make sure the ducklings had enough to eat and drink. He cupped one in his hand and brought it into the house. It was motionless. We knew it was dead. But Thom had a child's faith. He extended his hands up to Dad with the lifeless fuzz ball held tenderly.

"Fix it, Daddy."

Healing Crystals

Dad told me that when he was young, people all over the country bought crystals advertised to cure virtually every ailment. News of their healing powers traveled from neighbor to neighbor. The crystals worked! They worked wonders for people who suffered from headaches, bellyaches, backaches, congestion, gout, earaches, vertigo and obesity. You name it. The crystals had magical powers over disease.

It turned out that the crystals had no distinguishable active ingredients. How did they work? The instructions asked the purchaser to mix a small amount of crystals in a large glass of water. Perhaps yet another glass of water or two would help move the crystals to the point of disease.

Cured! Healed! Magic!

Americans simply failed to drink adequate amounts of water. Once one was properly hydrated, the partaker reported miraculous results.

Even today we could learn a few lessons from the healing powers of those glasses and glasses of watery crystals from the better part of a century ago.

Rescued from China

Brother Thom and I should be in China right now, thanks to Dad's 2.5 horse-power Elgin outboard motor. Dad loved to take us boys saltwater fishing for salmon in Puget Sound or the Pacific Ocean off the Makah Tribal town of Neah Bay on the northwestern tip of Washington state.

My earliest recollection sees Dad taking us fishing near Maury Island, across from where we lived at Covenant Beach in Des Moines, Wash. I was 7, and Thom was 4. I don't recall catching anything that afternoon, and the shadows lengthened. Darkness fell, and I could see Dad was concerned. We were lost. He and Mom helped build a chapel on the waterside of the Tabernacle, an old dance hall converted into a camp meeting auditorium.

That dark night on the water, Dad told us to pray that Mom would turn on all the lights in the chapel, so we could see the windows lit up along the water. Oh, I suppose we weren't in real danger. Dad could have headed our little 12- or 16-footer toward any light ashore and called for a rescue. Dad had a bit of a stubborn streak in him, and a touch of pride. He didn't relish putting us at the mercy of someone on the island, only to wait an eternity for a way home. How would he get the boat home? But he talked nothing of that. He just kept searching for a familiar landmark. But we were a long way from the mainland. Thom and I were cold and I think I was too scared to concentrate on praying.

Dad must have prayed, at least. Why would Mom ever think of turning on all the lights in the chapel? Something prompted her to switch them on, however, and when Dad saw them, he gave out with a little yelp. Homeward bound.

That wasn't the only time we were lost at sea.

Beyond Tatoosh Island off Neah Bay, Dad's tiny outboard putt-putted us into huge ocean swells. Nearby boats would appear and disappear behind the swells. The clouds threatened and turned angry.

"I think we should head in," Dad said. "It looks like a nasty storm is brewing." He opened the throttle of the Elgin and turned the miserably small boat around. Maybe 20-30 minutes later, that dreaded concerned look appeared on Dad's face.

"We're going backwards—the current is too strong for the motor, and it's taking us out to sea."

Swell.

I don't remember Dad signaling, but after what seemed like another eternity, the fishing crew of a cabin cruiser must have seen our plight. They pulled in front of us, threw us a line and towed us away from China.

Two-and-a-half horses on the rolling swells of the Pacific. That's enough adventure for me. My idea of roughing it, as Gene Neudigate says, is going barefoot in the Holiday Inn.

God's Cod

One of my favorite places to fish with Dad and Thom was at Pender Harbour, British Columbia, when we were kids. Dad found a secluded fishing resort with primitive cabins and small fishing boats with inboard motors. Want to go to the store? Hop in the boat—it was the only way to get there.

One day before our trip to Canada, I recalled someone driving me to a remote job site where Dad was working by a lake. He left two fishing poles on the bank with baited lines in the water. Later he took me down to the lake and we found two small trout on the end of the lines.

So, I figured, this should work just as well in the serene salt water Canadian harbour. I baited a hook at the end of the line on Dad's rod and reel, dropped the line into the water and balanced the rod across the tied-up boat.

A couple of hours later, Dad asked if anyone had seen his rod and reel. I had hoped to surprise him with a fish, and coaxed Dad down to the water. To my dismay, the rod was gone.

I told Dad what I had done and said someone must have stolen the gear.

"A fish probably pulled it in," Dad muttered. Impossible, I thought.

Dad took a large four-pronged anchor or hook of some kind and began dragging the bottom of the harbour.

I prayed. Fervently.

After what seemed like an eternity, Dad said, "You better hope we find it, or you'll have to buy a new rod and reel. That was my best gear."

I silently cried out to God.

After another 30 minutes or so, Dad decided to untie the floating dock and turn it around.

"I'll try one more time," he said.

I had nearly given up hope, but I still bombarded heaven with my desperate pleas.

When he pulled up the hook, a fishing line appeared. Dad grabbed it and pulled it onto the dock. A still-writhing rock cod had swallowed the hook.

My heart would nearly burst with praise to God.

It was a young man's first glorious memory of an answer to a prayer for an outcome considered impossible.

I do believe; help me overcome my unbelief! Mark 9:24b (NIV)

Navigating with the Mobility of Blind Faith

Carpoolian Mary Ann Kennedy teaches the sight-impaired. She tells of a blind woman who answered questions of curious children.

"When you were born, were you scared when you found out that you were blind?"

The woman patiently pointed out the riches of life she had discovered using her other senses.

"My only regret is that I can't drive," she told her young listeners.

More than a century earlier, blind Fanny Crosby wrote thousands of hymns, some of my favorites. She often wrote about what she could see with her mind's eye, and though she lost her sight in an accident, she found her blindness to be a blessing. As a young girl, she wrote the following:

> *Oh what a happy child I am, although I cannot see!*
> *I am resolved that in this world, contented I will be!*
> *How many blessings I enjoy that other people don't!*
> *So weep or sigh because I'm blind I cannot—nor I won't!*

When I was a boy, blind Walt Kraemer tuned and refurbished the piano I played at home.

"Show me where your electrical outlet is," he said. "I'll watch you, so I can find it myself next time."

He replaced all the ivory on the keys and tuned the piano with precision. He would love to tell lighthearted stories of what it was like to be blind.

"My wife and I started turning the lights on at night in our home," he said with a smile. "We don't need them, of course, but friends of ours stopped by and left, because they thought no one was home!"

Friend Jim Kluge is a paraplegic and often scorns the Americans with Disabilities Act—ADA—for requiring such things as Braille signs at drive-up banking windows.

Jim, you might reconsider.

Walt Kraemer drove. He told us he once lived in the country and he'd drive to the next farmhouse. He'd listen for the sparse traffic, and he knew where he was on the road by sensing the rise of the road.

My co-workers sometimes get the most outlandish inquiries about the Corps of Engineers.

"I can't *imagine* we are involved with that," they often say.

Walt Kraemer taught me otherwise.

Imagine.

Thanks Heaps, Mr. Patillo

Mr. Thomas Patillo was my fourth grade teacher, and our class was the envy of all the kids in school. Mr. Patillo would give us rides home, let different kids take the class guinea pig home, and he was the one who carried me and ran to the office after Tommy Blevins threw his bat and it hit me above the eye. Of course, we hung onto every word our revered teacher would say. We'd bring him huge delicious apples and he'd eat all but the stem. He said real Washingtonians ate the whole apple, core and all. I still do that today.

And since I digested every word coming out of Mr. Patillo's mouth, I must say he turned out to be something of a spoiler over the decades. One day, before a three-day weekend, we were all excited about the long break from school, until he tried to put things in perspective.

"Why bother with a three-day weekend," he said. "It will be over almost as soon as it starts." As always, he was right. Those three days, and every long weekend since, flew by—always far too short.

I found a remedy. Later in life, someone had told me the phenomenal difference in his life he discovered by fasting and praying. I had fasted before, but I hadn't focused on combining the two. I decided to give it a try. One evening after Air Force Reserve training, I was staying in the Bachelor Officers Quarters. I opted to skip dinner and got down on my knees next to the bed.

I prayed in detail for family, friends, associates, missionaries, pastors, the world, students, bosses, former co-workers, the president, cabinet, Congress, the military chain of command, the hungry, the lost, the lonely…. It was my intention to pray far into the night. After praying for what seemed like several hours, I peeked at my watch.

Twenty minutes had gone by. Well, I tried. I got up, turned on the TV and watched the news.

Mr. Patillo, I finally figured out how to counter your spoiler advice. I know how to make that weekend seem as long as I (or the devil) wants.

Tried and Tested Near Death

Bill and Lane James, two young kids next door, helped brother Thom and I build an underground fort. Lane, the younger, wasn't much help. He was always the brunt of our jokes—ever since Dad good-naturedly referred to a bunch of us as "you crazy guys" and Lane, offended, responded, "I'm not crazy; I'm just dumb."

We let Lane try to gouge the hard dirt a little. He'd give up quickly. After several hours, the rest of us had dug a couple square holes—the main rooms—and connected them with passageways.

Open at the top, we found old doors and plywood as roofs to our rooms and tunnels and shoveled a bunch of dirt on top, packing it down so it looked like the rest of the yard, but without grass. Some of the plywood bowed a bit when you walked on top, but our hideaway would fool most people—most young kids, anyway, we thought. We left only one small opening where we would lower ourselves into the musty fortress. We hadn't quite figured out how to solve the problem of near-total darkness down there. I guess we found some candles to suck up the scarce oxygen below.

Soon after we threw the last shovels of dirt on our creation, we were standing around imagining that no one could tell that we had crafted a wondrous maze of caverns beneath the earth.

Suddenly, the James boys' dad, Frank, showed up.

"Whatcha up to, boys?"

"Oh, nuthin'—we made this underground fort."

"Well, that's fine, boys, but these things can be dangerous. Before you use it, let me see how sturdy it is. We want it to be safe, so nobody gets buried alive!"

The burly man began jumping up and down on the springy plywood, loosening some of the dirt. We could hear creaks, and we feared that his monstrous bouncing weight would crush the roof and ruin our daylong project.

Just then, you could hear a faint, muffled blood-curdling holler.

Thom comes wriggling up through the opening with panic in his eyes. Not one to sass his elders, he brushed himself off, and we watched in disbelief, having witnessed a narrow escape from certain death.

I don't recall any of us ever going back into that chamber of horrors. Not long after that we used the plywood and doors for some other project—I think they became the roof to our above-the-ground clubhouse in the vacant lot next door.

The James' dad's rare and freak visit wasn't to be repeated, and we were glad that he never came around to ruin our world anymore. Prone to bickering and squabbling, we were perfectly capable of ruining our world—all by ourselves, thank you.

The Sneaky Sneeze

…you may be sure that your sin will find you out. Numbers 32:23 (NIV)

Dan, Don and I thought we got away with our tomfoolery in the back of Interbay Covenant Church. The pastor and congregation were focused on a rousing hymn-sing. We mischievous boys found the ultimate in entertainment, hidden in the back left corner of the church.

We giggled uncontrollably—and muffled by the singing—as we made ourselves sneeze repeatedly. How? We created an ingenious invention, the bobby-pin sneeze device. Tickling the inside of our noses with the device, we couldn't stifle a rousing sneeze. Again, and again and again. We could sneeze with impunity. The louder the singing, the louder the sneeze, followed by uproarious laughter. No one could see us. What fun! We'd sneeze to our heart's content.

Suddenly, Don's dad, the pastor, surprised us as we looked up and saw him standing at our side with a stern look of rebuke. While everyone else sang on, he said, "You boys are showing disrespect to God's House."

Where did he come from? Wasn't he leading the singing? Did God somehow tip him off?

End of sneezing. End of fun. Ditch the bobby pins. Time for sober reflection. God, indeed, even sees the sneeze.

> O LORD, you have examined my heart and know everything about me.
> You know when I sit down or stand up. You know my every thought when far away.
> You chart the path ahead of me and tell me where to stop and rest. Every moment you know where I am. You know what I am going to say even before I say it, LORD.
> You both precede and follow me. You place your hand of blessing on my head.
> Such knowledge is too wonderful for me, too great for me to know! I can never escape from your spirit! I can never get away from your presence! If I go up to heaven, you are there; if I go down to the place of the dead, you are there. If I ride the wings of the morning, if I dwell by the farthest oceans, even there your hand will guide me, and your strength will support me. I could ask the darkness to hide me and the light around me to become night—but even in darkness I cannot hide

*from you. To you the night shines as bright as day. Darkness and light are both alike to you. You made all the delicate, inner parts of my body and knit me together in my mother's womb. Thank you for making me so wonderfully complex! Your workmanship is marvelous—and how well I know it...*Psalm 139 (NIV)

Dan, Dave, Downtown, Don, Dogs and Dag's

My first recollection of Dan Koser was when he was in first grade. I was in second. I would see him at Interbay Covenant Church in a maroon pair of dress shorts and a matching hat. Even then he was a big kid, busy, sociable—a clown. I didn't really get to know him until I was in about fourth grade. He invited me over to his house. My folks dropped me off, and he greeted me with unrestrained squeals of delight and a bear hug. No one had ever greeted me with such enthusiasm. I was a shy, insecure kid, and it felt good, although I'm sure I was more reserved in my response. It was the beginning of a close, lifelong friendship.

I think I spent most of my childhood at Dan's house. We made a clubhouse in his musty dirt basement. We ran hours and hours of football up-over-and-up pass plays, though he often made fun of my uncoordinated performance. He good-naturedly beat me up, telling me it was for my own good, that it was toughening me up. Once he threw me down a long flight of stairs at church and laughed at the comical sight. He said that toughened me up as well. We acted in silly reel-to-reel taped comedy hours. Dan's sister Sharon encouraged us by laughing until tears ran down her face. Maybe I hung around because he was always feeding me. Side-by-side attached slices of bread with butter and brown sugar. Fresca ice cream floats. Every Saturday night Connie Mack Koser, Dan's dad, would gather the family in a circle and scoop ice cream out of a 3-gallon tub. Each family member looked forward eagerly to the occasion. But one day he called everyone together and said they could get their own ice cream out of the freezer—anytime they wanted. He thought he was being big-hearted. But no one liked ice cream as much anymore. Just wasn't the same.

I owe Dan a fortune. While I carried cheesy newspaper routes for $4-$7 a month—*Shopping News* and *Ballard News*—Dan carried the big-league morning daily, the Seattle Post-Intelligencer. His $30 monthly take burned a hole in his pocket, and I was the beneficiary. He paid my fare and food countless times to accompany him downtown, where he'd ogle toys and gadgets in the department stores. About 100 times he took me bowling. I was no match, but as a kid who was broke, I felt rich when I hung with Dan. Later, Dan and I buddied up with Don Dahlstrom, the preacher's kid, and his *Green Onion* Ford. I owe Don a fortune for my share of the gas and chow. Sometimes when we'd pull up to Dag's Beefy Boy Burgers I'd pretend I was asleep—no burger money. They knew better. "Harris, quit faking it." They bought me a 19-cent burger and shake.

To try to balance things out, I looked for bargains and promotions. Dan and I rode our bikes as young teens to a grocery store in Magnolia that celebrated its grand opening by selling foot-long hotdogs for a dime and burgers for a nickel. We went Dutch treat, and I thought I was a big spender. Imagine—paying my own way. Another time Dad took the two of us to the Home Show where he had an automatic garage door exhibit. Dan and I frequented the free 7-Up and Canada Dry booths and stood through the same blender demos to scarf down a couple dozen free samples of soup, veggie juice and frozen dessert. There was no end to my generosity that day.

Dan and I never got to go to elementary or junior high school together, but I convinced him and his folks for him to join me at King's High School, an inter-denominational Christian school 10 miles north of our home. I'll tell about those unforgettable years in other chapters.

One day the three D's—Dan, Don and Dave—were riding in the *Green Onion* on a snowy Sunday afternoon. Don wore a silly hat he found. THONK! Someone bombed the windshield with a snowball projectile. Don jammed the brakes and slid to a halt. Both doors opened and my compatriots ran toward the offending throwers. I didn't want any part of that and sat tight. The bombers turned out to be high school behemoths or college men. My buddies decided not to tangle with them and retreated to the car. Don was now bare-headed.

"Is this your hat, Sonny?" The bombers mocked their victims. Don's silly hat, we discovered, had belonged to a Cub Scout! Tails between our legs, we drove off silently and split a gut in self-mocking laughter when we were well out of sight.

He sold me an old '53 Ford for $100 that was totally gutless. When I tried to sell it to an older man, it wouldn't even climb Seattle hills. Needless to say, it was a tough sell.

Now, you ask, why would I hang with a guy that constantly assured that I had an abundance of pain? What did I see in someone who took sadistic pleasure in seeing me suffer? Well…a friend is someone who knows all about you and still loves you. Dan's parents were like another Mom and Dad to me. They thought of me as a son. Dan and I go back a half-century, after all. We plotted and schemed about girls, double-dated, worked side-by-side, played high school football together and served at the same time in the Armed Forces during the Vietnam era. Dan worked on my cars while I slept, picked me up at midnight on his scooter from GG's Broiler where I washed dishes (I would make him milkshakes), took me on his scooter 10 miles to high school, walked home with me the 10 miles when it was too late to call the folks after a game (I think we got home at 3:45 a.m.), shed tears with me and his folks when we went to a football reunion and heard about a miracle in his brother Norm's life (a coach told about Norm's "homecoming" after years of being a prodigal son, of sorts)…and then a teacher stood up, overjoyed by the news, saying he had prayed for Norm every day for, what? 20 years?

And then it was the bond we shared after our two dads died, not too far apart. Dan recalled how *the Spirit also helps in our weaknesses. For we do not know what we should pray for as we ought, but the Spirit Himself makes intercession for us with groanings which cannot be uttered.* He told me how he heard a deep, deep groan somewhere inside of him when he learned his dad had died on the operating table after suffering chest pains visiting daughter Sharon in Kentucky. When my dad died in 1994, Dan shared the feelings he experienced when his dad died. I wrote back:

July 25, 1994

Dear Dan,

What a powerful and moving letter you sent me. It met my need in a big way. Your description of hugging yourself on behalf of your Dad really hit the mark. And your reminder of the anointing.

Psalm 133:1-3 (NIV):

> *Behold, how good and how pleasant it is for brethren to dwell together in unity!*
> *It is like the precious ointment upon the head, that ran down upon the beard, even Aaron's beard: that went down to the skirts of his garments;*
> *As the dew of Hermon, and as the dew that descended upon the mountains of Zion: for there the LORD commanded the blessing, even life for evermore.*

I have felt a supernatural peace and calm, but since family started returning home, I've had my ups and downs. I miss Dad. I told God He could have him. And I wouldn't want to be selfish, because our two dads are so much better off. I had hoped and prayed that God would enable the sale of Dad's business, and that he would have many years of restful and joyful retirement, but it was not to be. He died exactly as he wanted to—with his boots on.

I found myself looking up, startled, several times when I saw an older gentleman, thinking he looked like Dad. I found myself fantasizing that it had all been a case of mistaken identity and that Dad would come walking in with a grin on his face. It was not to be.

When I came to work, I was greeted by a huge butcher-paper poster, signed by many people in the building, "From your Corps Family," with a beautifully calligraphed scripture:

Romans 8:38-39 (NIV):

> *For I am convinced that neither death nor life, neither angels nor demons, neither the present nor the future, nor any powers, neither height nor depth, nor anything else in all creation, will be able to separate us from the love of God that is in Christ Jesus our Lord.*

Beat up and bruised, Jesus and I still love Dan. Dan is my surrogate Dad. When Dad was alive, I called him, desperate, to say I had a pinhole leak in my water heater. "No problem," Dad reassured me. "Shut off the water. Drain it. Drill a tiny hole through the leak. Put a screw and washer there."

Dad cannot answer those questions today. My buddy Dan can. Dad can. Dan can. Dad...Dan. They sound a lot alike. And their mature, wise counsel and comforting words sound alike as well.

No pain, no gain. Because of Dan's athletic example, this former "93-pound weakling" ended up lifting weights, turning out for football and running up to 15-milers. I owe him a lifetime of memories. I'm quite certain he'll stick around until I repay those trips downtown and bowling marathons. Yes, Dan's a pain. A keeper—just like my back. It kills me on occasion. But I've grown attached to it, and when my back hurts, it motivates me to greater discipline, activity, empathy and compassion. My back cuts me no slack. It's real. It keeps me honest. Likewise, Dan, among my very closest of friends and family—he tells me like it is.

I wouldn't trade Dan's lessons in discipline for anything. He did his godly duty and taught me perseverance and undying friendship.

As iron sharpens iron, a friend sharpens a friend. Proverbs 27:17 (NLT)

Lethal Dare?

I couldn't afford the $3 tickets for my high school banquet, but I wanted to invite Mary Duncan or Lynda Kibbey. Don Dahlstrom to the rescue!

At a High League church party Sunday night, I had been drinking root beer and Cokes. Now Don had a dare, and I couldn't resist. He would pay for the banquet tickets if I would drink a gallon of water in a half-hour. Hey, I wanted to go to the banquet with everyone else. So I did it.

Gladys Gerdin came by later to pick up her daughters. Someone told her of the dare. "I know where you'll be sitting all night." Mothers with only daughters don't understand. I'll spare you the gruesome details, but I was up most of the night.

The next day at school, Mr. Mills, the science teacher, scolded me when he heard about it. He told me never to try that again. It could be fatal. Ever since then, for 40 years, my kidneys will hurt if I hold it in too long.

God had mercy on me. My kidneys hurt—seldom over the 40 years with proper attention—and I've never had any serious problems in the plumbing department. As abusive as I have been with my body—atrocious posture and diet—I feel great and today I'm the picture of health. Covert Bailey wrote *Fit, Not Fat*. Maybe I should write *Fit **and** Fat*. Suffering? There, but for the grace of God, go I.

"Bad" Boy

At King's Schools in the early 1960s, the pranks pulled by kids to break the rules were pretty mild stuff compared to today, for the most part.

King's high Christian standards turned some people off, but the administration's heart was in the right place. Today we complain about rap music that preaches murder and all manner of unimaginable rebellion. In the 1960s, King's didn't want us listening to rock 'n roll, going to movies, smoking, drinking or holding hands. Turns out the evangelicals were prophetic about the evils of some of that—smoking, for instance.

The school reluctantly decided *Ben Hur* was a possible exception, because it was biblically based. Ralph Kratzer, the band teacher, even ordered the *Ben Hur* theme music for band. The whole band showed up to chapel, each in his or her own seat, holding an instrument. Herman Bohl, the Bible teacher, and three other teachers shouted individual numbers from different sections of the chapel: "One! Two! Ready! Play!"

The band members stood up and belted out the movie music spectacular. It was one of the highlights of our school days, a bit edgy for that proper place.

Gary Slattery pulled a prank that got everyone charged up, though in most other schools it wouldn't raise an eyebrow. Seattle's number one rock station was KJR-AM. Pretty mild stuff by today's standards. You might hear *Love Me Tender, Purple People Eater* or *The Witch Doctor*: "Oo-ee-oo-ah-ah, Ting-tang-walla-walla-bing-bang…" Gary decided to buy an ad for KJR in the *King's Quill,* our student newspaper. In my subsequent senior year I shared editor duties with Loren Postma and Ron Richardson. I had nothing to do with ad sales.

Mrs. Rood was the newspaper advisor. She didn't bat an eye, so the staff moved forward with the ad. On the school bus, Gary even showed a letter around, a thank-you letter from KJR. I never heard if they kicked in any money for the ad.

Mrs. Rood must have jotted the call letters down. The night before King's Press would release the new edition, Mrs. Rood listened to the station. I'm not sure exactly what happened. I only know the result. Here's what I think happened. Mrs. Rood called the King's Press manager late that evening.

"Have you printed the *Quill* yet?"

"Yes."

"Oh, Dear. What would it take to reprint it?"

"You're talking about the expense of all new paper and new plates and perhaps a delay of a day or two."

"See what you can do about that awful KJR ad."

The next day we got the *Quill*. Right on time. Where the KJR ad was supposed to be were dozens of black wavy lines. I think the ink was still wet. If you pressed your hand on it, it turned black.

High standards meant that the slightest infraction got the student adrenalin pumping at top speed. It didn't take much to get a buzz going throughout those beloved hallowed halls.

Drugs? Who need them?

Remedy Worse
Than the Screw-Up

My summer work program of 440 hours at King's Garden brought me delights every day. King's built the most modern and powerful FM radio station on the West Coast, thanks to the savvy and committed radio engineer who designed it. I marveled at the studios with their intriguing control boards and microphones. My early introduction to the station likely inspired me to study radio-television later in college.

It was my privilege as a King's Garden kitchen worker to take a meal down to the announcer or engineer on duty at the station. One day I dropped the tray, and food and drink spilled all over the shiny concrete floor of the room that housed much of the transmitter equipment. I quickly looked around for something with which to clean up the mess before anyone discovered what I had done.

In the bathroom, I found a bucket with a mop and what appeared to be some pleasant-smelling brown water in a bucket. I squeezed out the mop, swabbed the deck and rinsed the mop in the bucket. Now the contents looked like muddy water mixed with milk and sickening-looking chunks of mystery meat and veggies. I flushed the whole mess down the toilet.

I was proud of my responsible action. I returned to the kitchen and fetched another tray of food.

The next day I noticed a Roto-Rooter truck outside the radio station.

It wasn't until much later that I pieced together the rest of the story. That brown liquid was floor wax. My pouring it down the toilet clogged up the sewer system but good.

Years later I sent King's a substantial check as my tithe for one of the months I was in Korea.

Subconsciously, I must have hoped the contribution helped cover the expense of unstopping the drain.

Minimum Wage

All kids think they have to work as slaves for free for their parents—never mind the room and board and full benefits. Other than that, I've not found anyone whose high school wage undercut mine.

I enjoyed one of life's greatest pleasures in working for and attending King's Garden High School. Son Mike also attended and graduated in 1986. It's more now, but his tuition was $300 a month. Mine? Back in the sixties it was around $225 a year.

Every high school student would agree with me: the best part was the summer. I worked hard during the summer—tearing out plaster in the girls' dorm, sweeping driveways and doing tons of dishes. King's Garden offered a work-study program allowing me and other students of limited means to work 440 hours and earn their full tuition for the upcoming year. As I recall, there were about 10-18 girls in the dorm and buddy Dan and I held down the boys' dorm for two summers.

King's decided 18 girls and two boys spelled potential trouble, so they appointed a recreational director. Not only did we have a date every night, but we got to go to the Aqua Follies on Green Lake, play a lot of softball and swim at Becky Judd's place—a property owned by King's on Echo Lake.

After 10 delightful weeks, the students went home. The administration approached Dan and me asking if we'd like to stay another week and do dishes before school started, since they still had a lot of Garden workers to feed. Dan thought he had had enough dishwater to last him another year. I initially questioned the going Garden-worker-child rate of 25-35 cents an hour, but my supervisor said a proposal awaited the Garden president's approval for a raise to 50 cents. I thought it over and decided I could use an extra $22 bucks, and I accepted.

It was the loneliest week of my life. Getting energy from other people, I found the week away from buddies and girls painfully dreary. Finally, the week was up and I went to Mrs. Kilgore's office to collect my pay.

"Not yet," she said. "It will be ready a couple weeks after school starts."

After what seemed an eternity, I again found Mrs. Kilgore, and this time she had a tiny cash envelope waiting for me. Eagerly I counted the one bill and a few coins—barely more than $5.

"There must be some mistake," I told her. Unfortunately, no.

"Since you were no longer on the work-study program, we took half your salary for room and board. And that proposal for a raise to 50 cents didn't go through."

Find someone who got less than 17-and-a-half cents an hour.

In retrospect, I'm delighted that happened. I've come to realize the priceless gifts King's Garden has given me over the years, not only in education, inspiration and spiritual guidance, but also in lifelong friendship. My beloved 66-student Class of 1962 remains very close, reuniting often, and looking forward to our 45th reunion in 2007. Other classmates share my view. A number have become authors, musicians, teachers, mechanics, missionaries, pastors and spouses of full-time Christian workers and my dear classmates have made a bold impact on the far corners of the world.

I am of all men most richly best, because Mrs. Kilgore, Mr. Hoy, Mr. Boyer, Mr. Nyquist, Mr. Judd, Mr. and Mrs. Postma, Mrs. Winquist, Mr. Inouye, Mr. and Mrs. Thiessen, Mr. and Mrs. Garcia, Dr. and Mrs. Lush, Mr. Kratzer, Mr. Staley, Mr. Rausch, Mrs. Swaney and all the other saintly King's Garden workers. They weren't working for their $40 to $120 a month salary. They had their eyes on the prize.

They were building a kingdom, and loving me into it.

Carpoolians, Bad Knees and Rooster Combs

Tom Mueller has led the life of Huck Finn, cruising down the Mississippi on a riverboat. He started with the Corps of Engineers in Seattle as a deckhand on the *W.T. Preston*, a majestic sternwheeler that picked up logs and navigation snags. Tom's not much younger than I and ran in track meets years ago. The carpool, going from work, waiting for the ferry and sailing home, is the place of the unwritten rule: you can say anything you want, politically correct or not, and what you say is not to be breathed outside the vehicle.

That's a way to find out the most intriguing things, the story behind the story about what's going on at work. Bonding happens. Some carpools are together for decades. Heidi, Tom's wife, first told me about her husband's adventures. I discovered later that she fulfilled my youthful dream of playing trombone in the University of Washington Husky Marching Band, and so I recruited her to help accompany the choir at the Corps' Seattle District Centennial, for which I wrote the Centennial song. Doug Graesser, husband of my co-worker Patricia, was also a member of the Husky Band. He didn't play for the Centennial, but Patricia sang in the choir, along with my mom, wife Suzanne, son Mike and daughter-in-law Polly. I directed. More about that later.

Tom is a fun-loving guy, left-leaning, who loves to goad me into lively discussions. In his wisdom, though, he won't take the discussion to the point of conflict leading to hard feelings. Instead, he tells me I'd have a tough time trying to hold my own with Heidi. "No one wins an argument with Heidi," he says. It's a boast that effectively calms the waters and turns the sailors to more pleasant talk for this trip, anyway. The peaceable ploy works miracles, because Heidi is rarely on the boat. She's off managing her public relations business.

I cannot tell you what Tom or driver Jack actually say in the carpool, but I can tell you that when you join, you will hear the most entertaining, sanctimonious pontifications on every topic imaginable. If I could just somehow, politely, persuade Jack to turn the droning National Public Radio down, so I could hear him

31

better. Jack chides me for my boredom with NPR. He asks if I prefer the news sound bites on AM radio.

My response: Choice. I told him I might not be interested in a 20-minute monologue on the tsetse fly in Borneo. Once I heard the dullest dissertation on the Marx Brothers. The sorry narrator told me there were four brothers: "Grouch Zeppo, Harpo and Chick-o." *Chick-o*??? He had written the script and couldn't even pronounce Chico's name. I suspect that many folks find NPR as dreary as I, but they listen because of peer pressure. It's an ideal tranquilizer. I was a student announcer at KUOW-FM, where NPR now resides in Seattle. The evolution of news often begins with radio, and then progresses to television, newspaper, weekly news magazine, book and, finally, a movie. One should get his or her news from a variety of sources, and the weekly news magazine may be the best source for in-depth reporting while offering choice.

I broke the carpool prohibition against divulging conversations but once. Carpoolian Mike Deering gave me ammunition to shoot down the awful concept of telework—sitting at home during office hours writing stories about sitting at home during office hours. Mike said his wife, Lori, had worked at home as a computer executive for years. She said sometimes she wanted to talk to someone besides their dog Boomer. My sentiments exactly.

But now, I can tell you the real reason I wanted to introduce you to Tom. Because Tom ran so many years in track, he ruined his knees. What the doctor prescribed for Tom's knees is what this chapter is all about. The remedy of note is *rooster's comb*. You heard me—that funny-looking floppy red thing hanging from a rooster's noggin. Grind the comb up and inject a solution of comb flakes into Tom's knees. Good to go. If that works, I'm all for it.

Here's my question. How did they think of that? Picture a bunch of physicians and lab technicians sitting around asking, "Well, we've tried ape cartilage and elephant brain. Nothing seems to relieve a messed-up knee. What can we try next?"

"I've got it!" A Coke-bottle-bespectacled geek in the back row jumps up, crowing. "The neighbor's rooster, Johnnie Cochran, drives me nuts. Has anyone ever tried ground-up rooster comb?" I'm sure we'll see a movie about this geek someday. What a beautiful mind, matching Johnnie's ugly comb with Tom's gnarly knees.

By and by, as fate would have it, Tom will have an opportunity to return the favor. I'm sure doctors will find they have in Tom a perfect match for an organ transplant to save the rooster's life. Maybe Tom would donate a kidney. He needs but one. Johnnie Crew-cut Cochran, you haven't seen the last of Tom. Keep your ear cocked.

Inspired Virtuosos
Echoing in My Mind

Pianos and organs have always fascinated me. Sitting with my folks toward the back of First Covenant Church (in case I yowled), the keyboard on the pipe organ looked like a white windowsill. I had no idea it had keys like a piano.

Perhaps three people influenced my interest in music—well, maybe four, if you count band teacher, Mr. Libby, at Catherine Blaine Junior High. Five, then. I wouldn't have been in the junior high band had Dad not played the trombone. Mr. Libby somehow got pimply-faced kids to produce a big brass band sound, and I was enthralled.

Before that, Miss Cedarholm, in fourth grade, asked for young pianists to audition to accompany the Lawton School band. I played mostly by ear, and I was an utter audition failure, as were a couple of my classmates. The pianist was selected, and the also-rans, like me, were offered the percussion section, since we supposedly understood rhythm. I took up the snare drum. Though I practiced hard for two years, my classmates laughed at me in sixth grade, and since I was a klutz, I knew I'd never be a drummer. They laughed because when I'd attempt a drum roll, I learned later to my horror that my head gyrated from side to side.

Well, I tried to play drums in junior high, but the skill level left me wanting. Dad still had his trombone, and I had had a few lessons in piano to be able to read one or two notes at a time. I got myself a beginning trombone instruction book and taught myself, then switched instruments in the junior high band. Mr. Libby could play just about any instrument. He heard me struggling, stopped the music and strolled over to me. With a twinkle in his eye, he picked up Dad's trombone and wiped off the mouthpiece. I anticipated he'd play my part flawlessly, but not before he let out with an ear-piercing blast. Startled, I saw my glasses flying across the room. That was the highlight of my junior high musical experience.

Ok, six influential people. Around age 8, Mom taught me a little ditty on the piano, using mostly black keys and two chords. I started picking out other melodies using those basic chords and figured out a couple more. I played most hymns by ear, using mostly black keys. Church musician Dorothy Belle King observed and said I was playing in six sharps. Since so many black keys were involved, it turned out to be six flats as well. So Mom got me started. I taught myself to transpose six sharps (or flats) into mostly white keys, the key of C.

Mom and Dad thought my playing by ear should undergo training, so they signed me up for piano lessons with Mrs. Thomas, a Japanese-American who married an Army officer. I learned where the notes were on the staff, but I lacked the discipline to progress very far. I got tired of simplistic melodies or two-note harmony, and I'd improvise my own.

Then, at King's, Ralph Kratzer was band teacher and an incredibly talented organist. He combined sight-reading and the ear in a marvelous way. I tried to emulate him. I bogged down at sight-reading, but Ralph wrote arrangements, and I started writing harmony for our brass quartet. One Christmas break I was bored, and so I bought a bunch of sheet music and wrote a composition for band. I was rather shy and self-conscious, and so I called it *Futility*. Ralph and the choir teacher, Bob Staley, decided to have me conduct the band in my composition at a recital.

Practicing didn't help my self-consciousness. All the cool girls played in the woodwinds section, and they couldn't keep from giggling constantly as I waved my arms. I turned around to see if I was properly zipped. I couldn't be totally sure without being obvious about it. But Neta, Heather and Becky kept bursting out in laughter. I finished the session and asked Neta what was so funny.

"Nothing too terrible," she said. Small comfort.

When I got home, I went to the bathroom and waved my arms in front of the mirror. That's it! I was wearing a pullover shirt that was a bit short on me. Each time I raised my arms to conduct the band, my belly-button peeked out. Mystery solved.

Darrell Rodman also inspired my interest in music at King's. He could write great arrangements, sight-read a concerto for piano, or listen to a record of a concerto and replicate it by ear. He also could improvise unlike anyone I had heard.

One Christmas someone asked me to write a vocal arrangement for the sextet to sing at the All School Banquet. I wrote the harmony in fifths for *Angels We Have Heard on High*. I heard Bonnie Burns practicing it with someone, and while I was flattered, it sounded a bit like Chinese music to me. I worried that the performance would flop.

At the banquet, Darrell's piano accompaniment was extraordinary. He made that sorry arrangement sound like heaven. Afterward, classmate Chuck Bennett enthusiastically congratulated me.

"That's the best arrangement you have ever put together," he said. No. It was the worst. But like God can do in making something beautiful out of a ruined life, Darrell made the song sound like a Broadway production.

Whatever happened to young Darrell, the virtuoso? Everyone said he should join us at Seattle Pacific College to pursue and refine his musical training. But like so many geniuses, he apparently knew more about how to put together a concerto than his teachers, and he flunked out. Last I heard, he joined the Christian musical group, the Spurlows, who later changed their format to sing to high school kids in a motivational program sponsored by Chrysler.

Many years later I took Dad and Mom to an exhilarating concert at Christ Memorial Church where the Azusa Pacific University choir and orchestra performed for the evening. The conductor kept singers on their toes by announcing different soloists or ensembles on the spot—all singers had to be ready for the sudden appointments.

The musicians sang a variety of styles, but one number featured an impromptu duet in which two young women belted out a classical performance that ultimately brought the audience to their feet. During the piece, Dad was overwhelmed. He turned to me lamenting how few young people ever hear this quality of masterful singing. During an uplifting crescendo, Dad turned away from me, engulfed in tears. The angelic sounds touched him deeply.

Shortly after that I was privileged to write a song to celebrate the Army Corps of Engineers' Seattle District Centennial. I chose the tune of *Wonderful Grace of Jesus* because of its rousing march-like cadence, and the words came out like this:

Seattle District Centennial Song

One hundred years of service
To the Pacific Northwest—
Serving the public purpose,
Putting our skills to the test

Achieving all our assignments,
Willing to try our best;
We're the lifeblood of Se-at-tle District;
Leading the rest!

CHORUS: Corps of Engineers' Seattle District,
Mighty feats throughout the great Northwest!
Model for the nation,
Landmark celebration,
Quality of legacy our quest!
We respond when neighbors call and need us,
Fighting floods until the skies are fair;
A heavy trust we're bearing,
Caring, daring,
Always there!

Achieving what the public asks us—
America's engineer!
Partners in problem-solving,
Overcoming, we persevere.

Stewards of waters and homeland,
Designs with that aligned;
We work for the next generation's
Future in mind!

Computer guru Dale Bryant copied the notes out of a hymnbook into a digital music device and produced sheet music for the event. We had a big picnic at the Ballard Locks, with brass and choir. We passed out a copy of the music to all the attendees, and practiced it once before the program began.

An elderly man approached the music stand. I asked him if I could help him. He held a copy of the music, and he pointed out where there should be a natural and where there was a sharp instead of a flat. How did he know? I asked myself.

"And I know this man's parents," he said, pointing to my name on the sheet.

"Who are you?" I asked.

"My name is Winston Johnson." O my.

"Winston, I was a camper in your cabin decades ago at Covenant Beach."

Professor Johnson, in his eighties, remembered the raucous cabin full of energetic boys.

"Do you know that four of those boys went on to become pastors?" He then went on to name them all.

Winston came with Cindy Wikstrom, a Corps worker who is Winston's niece. I took him over to talk to Mom, who was there as part of the choir.

Winston had been organist at that pipe organ at First Covenant Church when I was a boy, and later at University Presbyterian.

But I remember him most for an extraordinary organ recital when he taught at Seattle Pacific College. He played a fast-moving and intricate number that captivated the audience. It was exhausting to perform, and when he finished, sweat poured from his brow. He stood up and took a bow to thunderous applause, a standing ovation.

My mouth hung open as I realized that they weren't flying fingers that enthralled us. Faster than Fred Astair, he produced most of the fastest and complex melody not with his hands.

But with his feet.

Is There One Person in Seattle Who Hasn't Worked at Boeing?

Dad hated Boeing. He'd only work there if business was bad and he wanted to eat. But he'd stay there no more than maybe six months. He couldn't stand the bureaucracy. He worked as an inspector on the prototype 707 passenger jet aircraft. They'd beg him to stay, offering him promotions. Not on your life.

A couple years later, when he was hungry enough, he'd hold his nose and go back to Boeing. He chose the graveyard shift because he could work midnight until 6:00 a.m. and get paid for eight hours. He'd try to sleep during the day, but brother Thom would go down to the dirt basement, Dad recalled, step on some records and put one of them on an old fashioned crank phonograph. Dad said he'd go to work that night singing, "Green for go; red for stop; be your own little traffic cop..."

Years later Boeing laid off Dad's engineer friend, Les Hedeen. Eighteen months later, they called Les back. The same letters were still in his in and out baskets.

So, when I graduated from college, what did I do? I spotted a closed circuit TV system on a visit to Boeing one day, and since I majored in radio-television at the University of Washington, I visited their white-collar employment office and asked if I could work in their TV department. The personnelist never heard of it and sent me downstairs to the blue-collar employment office. Down there, they told me I was overqualified with my degree and sent me back upstairs. I went back and forth for a week, until Boeing Fire Chief Con Koser, my buddy's dad, appeared.

"What are you doing here, Dave?"

I told him my yo-yo experience with the two employment offices.

"Hey, I know all these personnel guys. Let me talk to them." He disappeared into the white-collar office. Ten minutes later, the personnel guy called my name. I was hired. One hundred thirty dollars a week. Start Monday as a Program, Evaluation Review Technique Scheduler-Planner Industrial Engineer on the 747 project, still on the drawing boards.

I hustled home and told my father in law my new title.

"What's the title of the top guy at Boeing?"

"President?"

"And the next guy down?"

"Vice President?"

So, what you're saying is that the longer the title, the lower down in the organization you are."

I was glad for the job, being about to be married, and they issued me a blue-top badge. Supervisors had orange-top badges.

I kept hearing names being paged over the loud speaker. Someone told me you could call a number, page someone, and they'd announce, "Johnson...Ralph Johnson." Then Ralph was to call his office.

Some guy had been passed over for promotion several times. He paged himself every 15 minutes for three months. Soon after that, he was promoted! Name recognition.

Boeing built a brand new building at the Renton plant where I worked for awhile. They poured a new sidewalk. A week later they jack-hammered the sidewalk and laid conduit.

I've tolerated federal bureaucracy for 37 years only because of my roots. Boeing was far worse.

Big Fans of the Techies

Dad worked aboard his Coast Guard ship, sweltering in the tropical heat of the Philippines during World War II. He was the electrician, and working fans were worth more than gold and in short supply. He set his priorities, but there just weren't enough hours in the day to keep all the electrical systems running.

Fresh fruit was a rare treat aboard ship. But the cooks were desperate. They begged Dad to come and fix the galley fan before the crew melted.

"Pssst. Bob. Fix the fan and this is yours."

Through a hatch came a big box of beautiful fresh oranges. Dad thought for a moment. Priorities weren't locked in. He quickly got the fan running and took off with the oranges. He didn't drink. He never bought a round of "cheer." But that night, he offered his buddies something much more in demand. Enjoying the cool breeze of another of Dad's fans, the sailors found the juice of the oranges tasted sweeter than wine.

The Skipper was tough. He loved to pull surprise white-glove inspections. Several days later he had everyone suit up in their whites and stand by for inspection. Dad had just fixed the fan in the Old Man's cabin, but he was sweating bullets this time. His electrical shop was in shambles. After I came along I never knew Dad to be a shop neat nick. He had a bit of an "attitude" about the military, and sprucing up his shop was last on his list of priorities. Yet, here came the Old Man, wreaking havoc by running his white-gloved finger down "gig rails," finding the ever-present dust and intimidating the knee-knocking sailors. The Skipper himself could keep cool. He had one of Dad's fans. He came closer to the electrical shop. Stopped. Moved briskly to the shop hatch. He opened it a crack without turning on the light. Dad gulped.

"Very good." The Old Man moved on to his next target without even the slightest glimpse of Dad's Fibber McGee closet. He knew to leave well enough alone if he valued an uninterrupted cool breeze in the Captain's cabin.

In this century, Shannon Chenoweth, who was our crafty budget technician in the Corps of Engineers, came from the same mold as the galley crew. We can't function without computers, and computer techs are in short supply. Shannon's the best cook in the building. She makes sure the techie knew first-hand of her culinary delights.

As a result, we always had a well-fed computer techie hanging around, and we had the best-runnin', hummin' computers in the Corps.

Crying Colonel Caper

One of my public affairs officer predecessors for the 93rd Bombardment Wing at Castle Air Force Base, Calif., was a legendary lieutenant apparently fed up with make-work silliness on the home front during the Vietnam era. He liked to push the envelope on security and rules. He deemed gate security a joke and he was proven right. The lieutenant was convinced that he could drive a truck up to the gate with a picture of a round black bomb, a lit fuse and the word "Explosives" written on the side, and the guards would wave him right through. I don't know if he tried it.

What he did try apparently succeeded. A pesky lieutenant colonel came to see him every week. The ranking officer was in charge of the Base Beautification Program, and he wanted the junior PAO to write a weekly progress report for the base newspaper, the *Valley Bomber*. The younger officer quickly grew tired of warming up the same old news that his senior had planted young palm trees all around the perimeter of the parade field, decorating the large expanse of grass people would see as they entered the main gate.

How could he put an end to these dreary reports? He concocted a plan. Our public affairs office had its own photo lab. Around midnight, the lieutenant let himself in, picked up a quantity of liquid "hypo" chemical photo developer, and carefully poured a few ounces on each of the young palm trees. The senior officer never found out why they all died. End of the Base Beautification Program. End of the weekly progress reports. It was not, however, the end of the base security problems.

Two teenage members of the Civil Air Patrol decided to go on a joy ride one afternoon. They hopped in a hotrod that one of them owned, showed their CAP identification to the gate guard and headed for the bomb squadron. Inside the building, they walked into the locker room. One of the boys put on a flight suit with the silver leaf insignia of a lieutenant colonel. The other boy donned a major's flight suit. The major's suit hung by a couple flight caps, but the lieutenant colonel suit had no flight cap with it. Both boys put on the major's caps. Outside in the parking lot, they found a blue Air Force van with the keys in it. They drove it out the front gate and saluted the guard, who noticed that one of the

43

"officers" had silver leaves on the flight suit, but a gold leaf on his cap. He dispatched a patrol to chase them down, and the boys were apprehended in short order. When confronted, the young "colonel" began to cry.

End of story? No. A Merced *Sun-Star* reporter visited PAO every Tuesday to see if there was any news on his beat. "Not this week," the PAO said, but then the reporter heard a couple public affairs specialists talking with amusement about the boys who were caught.

Headline the next day: "Crying Colonel Caper." The Associate Press picked it up as a lighthearted "stinger," and it ran in the *Washington Post*. Security is no joke, especially when the brass read about it at the Pentagon. End of assignments for the Wing Commander, the Base Commander and the PAO. That's how I ultimately got the PAO's job.

(The *Sun-Star* is where we went down once a week to publish the base newspaper. One day an Asian American walked in and said, "I want to speak to Wally Palmer." Told there was no one at the *Sun-Star* named Wally Palmer, the man became insistent. Finally, when he demanded to put an ad in Wally Palmer, someone said, "Oh, you mean *Valley Bomber*.)

Rules of Engagement

Not long after the "Crying Colonel Caper," security tightened further. Another lieutenant colonel—rumor was that he was a recovering alcoholic—was "kicked upstairs" after a stint with the bomb squadron. He became administrative officer for the quiet little 47th Air Division Headquarters, a tenant on our base. The Division Commander was a brigadier general who created a stir by disguising himself as an airman basic and reporting to the main gate at night, saying he was newly assigned. Apparently he didn't feel adequately welcomed or properly guided to someone who could orient him to his "new home," and the general stirred things up to provide a warm welcome to future airmen.

The general and his staff often traveled to three or four other bases to provide inspections. He took his admin officer. One day they decided to inspect our base. As part of the in-brief, the senior leadership provided the general and his staff with a Top Secret overview in the command post, guarded by an airman with an M-16. The admin officer had become distracted and was late to the briefing. The door was locked. The guard was told not to let anyone in, standing grim-faced in front of two-way glass and beaming spotlights. What was the tardy admin officer to do to make himself useful for the duration? Ah! He approached the airman, who was decked in his "SP" guard uniform, and shouted, "Airman! What would you do if I did this?" Suddenly the officer grabbed the airman's rifle out of his hand.

"All due respect, Sir, I would do this." Without hesitation the airman doubled his fist and decked him.

The officer awoke on the floor a few minutes later and saw stars as he looked into the eyes of his general.

The double-fisted airman? They honored him with a medal.

No Chopsticks for a Formal Japanese Meal

I was one of the Misawa Air Base senior staff, and the Japanese governor included me among the Air Force invitees to his annual banquet before watching the festival parade as his guests.

The military staff struggled to remember their manners and bowed numerous times in attempt to keep up with our host's bows, not to mention those of his entourage. Then we sat down to the fanciest place settings I had ever seen. On three sides of the plate were perhaps more than a dozen pieces of silverware. A number of formally attired waiters scurried around pouring tea and serving dishes of food.

The Americans watched…and waited…and watched…and waited, keeping a bewildered eye on the Japanese dignitaries.

They smiled. We smiled.

More waiting, and watching and smiling.

Finally, the governor, with a scowl on his face, picked up one a spoon—why that one?—and awkwardly began to consume his soup. We followed suit. We managed to sample the rest of the meal with everyone looking nervous and wishing they were somewhere else, like in a hot tub.

I had taken my interpreter, Mickey, but he was seated near the colonel and governor, and he was out of earshot. Afterward, I mentioned to Mickey how difficult it was knowing which piece of silverware to use, and watching the Japanese wasn't much help.

"I know," he said. "They ordered the place settings to be arranged in formal American style. I noticed the Japanese dignitaries were of little help to you.

"They were waiting for you to show them which spoon to grab first."

That wasn't the first incident of cross-cultural misunderstanding. The colonels often came down to the public affairs office and asked Mickey to translate a brochure or thank-you note. The Vice Wing Commander had dropped off an Asian calendar for Mickey to translate.

Three weeks later, I noticed Mickey laboriously working on it.

"Mickey," I asked, "why is that taking so long?"
"It's in Chinese."

Super Secret (Keep It to Yourself, Please)

I've sat in on a number of classified secret briefings in working for the Air Force and Army. They might cover something as silly as getting to work after a nuclear bomb has vaporized the neighborhood—I still don't know how to do that—to classified operations during a military attack.

Overseas, a secret briefing might be a part of every senior staff meeting with the commander. The intelligence officer would spend the week poring over information from myriad sources. The commander wanted us to be situationally aware. Hostile or tense situations in certain parts of the theater during the Cold War may alter our flight training plans or weapon loads.

In Japan, where I lived on the northern tip of Honshu, the situation remained relatively stable, but the North Koreans not too far away had captured the crew of the Navy's U.S.S. Pueblo, causing international concern and my eventual deployment to South Korea.

I don't remember much about the secret briefings in Japan. One stands out, however. The intelligence officer, a captain, startled the commander with a report of a bizarre turn of events in the region.

Shocked, the commander asked, "What is your source for that information?"

The captain nervously shuffled through a curled stack of briefing papers. To his relief, he found the source of the secret revelation.

"CBS Evening News last night, Sir!"

A Message from MARS

When I was stationed without my family at Kunsan Air Base, Korea, in 1971, the Air Force tapped into something called MARS—Military Affiliate Radio Service. Staffed by airmen volunteers and designed for emergency use by the military, this transmission system would allow me to call an operator on base who would patch me into a ham radio operator in the States. The ham would call your wife and connect you. All the serviceman had to pay was the long-distance call from the ham radio location in the States to where one's wife resided.

The connection was tentative and full of static. It was difficult to hear my wife and when we began the transmission, our operator instructed us to say "over" at the end of each statement.

She and I talked for a minute or so and the connection was getting worse. I could hear a faint voice cutting in and out.

Somewhat exasperated, I raised my voice and asked, "What did you say, over?"

I heard nothing but the shhhhhhhh of static.

"I don't hear you. What did say…over?"

Just then the stateside ham operator broke into the conversation with a Brooklyn accent and ended the conversation by repeating her words. It just wasn't the same as hearing it directly and, well-meaning as it was, it left me feeling lonely, isolated and all the more distant.

"She sez she luvs ya!" Shhhhhhhhhhhhhhhhhhhhh.

If I Never See You Again

Charlie Ventimiglia, especially when he shaved his head, looked and sounded like Curly of the Three Stooges. He was the munitions squadron commander at Kwang Ju Air Base, Korea. Charlie loved to play practical jokes. Some of them weren't very nice, but we hesitated in retaliating, because Charlie announced he would retaliate 10-fold.

His favorite practical joke was to grab a CO_2 fire extinguisher, kick your barracks room door in, and spray "smoke" all over you and your room. Very funny. I was rather shy when I arrived at Kwang Ju and I spent most of my evenings writing letters and reading scripture in my room. Some of the other guys played Hearts down the hall in a little lobby. One evening I noticed liquid slowly advancing under my door. It was Charlie, trying to smoke me out so I would join them at play. I was amused, opened the door, laughed, and it was the beginning of a year-long friendship with Charlie and his buddies. He named everyone in the barracks after an animal. One captain, of Polish descent, he named the Pole Cat. Because I spent so much time in my room, Charlie told me he had named me the Possum. He told me he thought I was hanging by my tail from the ceiling.

Against my upbringing, I joined the group in playing the Hearts card game for a penny a point. A United Church of Christ Chaplain was one of those playing with us. Mom told me she didn't approve of playing cards—unless, perhaps, it was Flinch, Uno or Rook. But there was something about the symbolism in playing cards that wasn't kosher. But played I did. I wasn't very good at it. The object was to get rid of the queen of spades. One day I discovered why God and Mom disapproved of playing cards. I sloughed off the queen of spades with no regard as to who got it. The other players wanted it to count against the player who was ahead. I was just trying to get rid of it, and it went to the wrong guy. O my. The chaplain blew up. He screamed at me. He wouldn't speak to me for a week. I hated that card game for a long time after that. Mom was right. Eh, I always knew that chaplain was a radical, anyway. A good evangelical chaplain wouldn't blow up. Why not? Because he wouldn't be playing that nasty game! I don't mean to say that evangelicals don't have their flaws. I certainly do. Skeptics put down evangelicals and say they put everyone on a guilt trip. Untrue. God's Word provides not only awareness of guilt, but also, gladly, the solution of repentance and *joy in your presence, with eternal pleasures at your right hand.* Psalm 16:11 (NIV) That's no pie in the sky. For me that's already begun.

One of Charlie's practical jokes involved getting into a captain's refrigerator, squeezing condiments all over his door and, well, passing water on the mess. Charlie wasn't the most pleasant fellow, and yet at times he was a lot of laughs. My only regret was that if it were up to me to show him the light, I tried and failed. Yes, folks did weird things in Korea, but please understand, Dear Reader, that it was no fun being separated from family and loved ones for a year.

Perhaps the most memorable time with Charlie was at the end of our tours. He refused to go to a farewell party honoring him, and so we coaxed him into going by saying it was a party for me. I found a fire extinguisher full of water. I made a speech at the officers club saying that even though the party was for me, we wanted to honor Charlie. We had put up with his fire-extinguisher raids all year, and it was time for him to have a taste of his own medicine. I began spraying the water toward him. He dove under the table. I continued. Two other captains, laughing, ran into the other room looking for more fire extinguishers. They started spraying Charlie from another angle.

Charlie suddenly pressed his hands against his eyes. Something was dreadfully wrong. The flight surgeon quickly pulled Charlie into a janitor's closet and placed his head under a faucet, running water on his eyes. Those other fire extinguishers contained acid. The physician called for an ambulance and took Charlie to the clinic, where he examined Charlie's eyes under ultra-violet light. He swabbed the eyes with some kind of base goop, and called for an air-evac. Charlie was to be flown to a hospital at the other end of the country in Soule.

I felt terrible. After awhile, I walked back to my room, having heard that Charlie's eyesight was in jeopardy. As I approached my door, there was a large note stuck in the door with a Bowie knife:

HARRIS—IF I NEVER SEE YOU AGAIN, IT WAS NICE KNOWING YOU.

CHARLIE

Mom always said knock off the horseplay, or someone will get hurt.

I prayed.

Charlie sees.

World's Crying Need—
Plain English

If I were running for president and Dan Rather asked me what the most pressing crisis on earth is today, I wouldn't hesitate. It is the millions of baffling instruction sheets and manuals written in broken English by those who are fluent in a foreign language.

When I talk in the vanpool about something I heard on a late-night TV show, without exception I am told, "Oh, I couldn't stay up that late."

Neither can I. I videotape the show.

"Oh, I don't know how to program my VCR."

I'm the only guy over 15 who can. And that's only because I lived in Japan and Korea. I understand broken English communicated by my Asian friends.

If I become a millionaire in retirement, it will be in writing instruction manuals with an unusual twist—clarity.

When I lived in Korea, I visited the rather large city of Iri. In an attempt to attract more tourists, the city fathers decided to spend tens of thousands of their hard-earned *won* to publish a slick magazine in English. They assigned the task of composing the English to some poor guy who thought he had the language down pretty well.

It was a beautiful magazine with heavy, quality paper. On the front cover was a beautiful picture of the city. Emblazoned on the cover was the title carefully chosen to capture the spirit of the hospitable city.

"Iri—a city to live everybody."

Let Them Remember Their Misery No More

One of my warmest memories on an isolated one-year tour in Korea was Tuesdays. Several of us would knock off work at the air base at noon. We'd drive over to the Presbyterian missionary compound, spend the afternoon playing tennis, and then enjoy a fun-filled evening of supper, singing and a Bible study.

The Presbyterians practiced quite a bit more conservative lifestyle there than I had observed of them in the States. And for one thing, they allowed no alcohol on the compound.

The staff ran a hospital on campus, and they'd love Air Force guys to give blood. They said our blood was so rich they could use it for several Koreans.

One Christmas the hospital administrator, a retired soldier who paid his own expenses with his Army pension, pulled Air Force Chaplain Bob Tripp and me aside and invited us into his and his wife's apartment.

He offered us some eggnog, and it was quite tasty. We could detect that it had quite a kick to it, but that puzzled us, knowing the prohibition against alcohol.

The administrator revealed a mischievous smile. He said he understood the liquor ban, but then he led us in a little Bible study in Proverbs 31, beginning with verse 4:

It is not for kings, O Lemuel—not for kings to drink wine, not for rulers to crave beer, lest they drink and forget what the law decrees, and deprive all the oppressed of their rights. Give beer to those who are perishing, wine to those who are in anguish; let them drink and forget their poverty and remember their misery no more. (NIV)

I won't tell anyone if you won't.

Bang-Clang-We-Want-Chow!

When sisters Kathy and Laurie were in high school and grade school (there were 7-year intervals in our ages), I came home from the Air Force at Thanksgiving. Someone got mixed up and invited my folks to Thanksgiving dinner, but the invitation didn't include sons or daughters.

"No problem," I said. "I'll take the girls to Thanksgiving dinner at McChord Air Force Base in Tacoma." The girls came up short on the enthusiasm. I figured they were disappointed they couldn't go with the folks.

We borrowed a vehicle from Mom and Dad to drive from Covenant Beach, Des Moines, to McChord, about 30 miles away. The girls quietly rode in the back seat, bummed out. Adding to the gloom, we had car trouble on the road but managed to get it going.

Arriving at McChord and getting through security, we entered the chow hall, which the Air Force euphemistically likes to call the "dining facility." I had experienced holiday meals on military bases before, but the girls' wide-eyed expressions told me they were astounded at what they saw: beautiful, huge ice carvings of praying hands and a swan, tables for four with white tablecloths and a succulent turkey-and-ham dinner with every trimming and side dish you could imagine. After we said grace, the girls chattered happily over their scrumptious meal. On the way out, sharp-looking uniformed sergeants handed out bags of fruits and nuts. It was nothing less than first-class in every respect. On the way home, Kathy and Laurie kept up the lively chatter.

"What did you think, girls?"

"That was cool," they said. "Neat-o!"

"Why were you so reluctant to go?"

"Oh, we thought we'd have to sit at a long wooden table with a bunch of grungy soldiers in fatigues. We figured we would hear them banging tin cups and hollering, "We want chow.""

I could see as a public affairs officer that my work was cut out for me to change the public image of the modern Air Force.

The Other 'Gift' of More Sleep

You can call John and Shirley Schmidt angels sent from God. After an interminable 12 months' separation from my family while I was in Korea in 1971, I was stunned by the news that I would need to relocate to Fairchild Air Force Base in Spokane, now to suffer unexpectedly from a failed marriage and *Alone Again, Naturally*, as the song went.

I sought consolation at First Covenant Church downtown. John and Shirley welcomed this newcomer and learned I was an unaccompanied serviceman. Out of the goodness of their heart they invited me to Sunday dinner at a nearby restaurant. The conversation lasted some three hours as I poured out my heart over my painful loss.

They provided a powerful dose of understanding and encouragement. But, quite apart from my own troubles, I learned an important lesson from John on that comforting day of rest. In the course of the conversation he told me he had sought his master's degree by going to classes at night while working 40 hours a week. Returning from class each night, he studied the night away. He allowed himself only about two hours of sleep a night.

One night he noticed something that astounded him. John found he could read and retain material as fast as he could turn the pages of a complex textbook. His eyes raced down each page and upon reflection, he remembered close to 100 percent of what he had read over the past hour or more.

As it happened, he had been scheduled for a routine physical examination the next day. He hadn't planned to mention his reading discovery to the doctor, but somehow it came up in the conversation. John told him his new "gift" could accelerate his completion of academic requirements. Cool!

"How much sleep do you get during an average night?"

"Two hours."

"Stop it! Alter your schedule and start getting a good night's sleep every night," the doctor ordered with alarm. "Your 'gift' is a sure indicator that you are close to a nervous breakdown.'"

Needless to say, John delayed his graduation and cut a few more "Z's" on his way to earning his advanced degree.

The Best is Yet To Come

Rev. Gilbert Otteson was still going strong in his eighties and nineties as one of the best preachers I ever heard. He was devoted to his little blue-haired wife, Judith, who suffered from dementia. He waited on her hand and foot, all the while delivering powerful sermons. I still remember the message he delivered at the conclusion of the Vietnam War. He recited poetry and painted imagery of previous wars and the sacrifices of now dead soldiers.

Judith would say anything that came to mind. If Rev. Otteson would offer you the benefit and comfort of his substantive wisdom, Judith would saunter over and quietly tell you, "He's lying, you know."

One day, the couple was honored at perhaps their 60th wedding anniversary. Someone asked the Reverend what their most pleasant memory was as man and wife.

He provided the most gracious answer I've ever heard.

"We haven't had it yet."

Airhead's Tickled, Intuitive Alphabet Soup Perceptions

Popular seminar leader Bill Gothard taught, "What you practice in moderation, your children will excuse in excess." That principle could apply to Dad's humor as it relates to mine. Dad always had a quick comeback or original quip to life's quirks. Often he mimicked one of his friends or clients: "If it ain't the door, it's the telephone!" Many of his sayings or nicknames became family classics: "No brains!" "Green-and-yellow bucks," "nose nuggets," "PCBs (peanut butter popcorn balls)," "Bigfoot," "Fat Boy," "CW Fats (Covenant Women's Auxiliary)," "Glad-Eyes (Gladys)"or "Howlies (wild fringe groups at camp)."

Inheriting his genes, I not only look like him, but I had his knack of seeing the odd-ball and fun ways of looking at life. Someone said to Suzanne, "Your husband is quite the wit." Her response: "You're half right." Unfortunately, especially in my younger years, my humor clearly dipped into overkill. My humor was overdone, in a relentless pursuit to see practically everything in its absurd aspects. Someone once asked comedian Steve Allen where he got all his spontaneous material. "There's never a shortage of material," he explained. "The problem is editing it before it comes out of my mouth." I know the feeling.

Me: "Honey, two nights ago I dreamt I was a wigwam, and then last night I dreamt I was a teepee."

Suzanne: "You're just two tents." This is a story that sounds better than it reads.

Humor must be clean from Dad's perspective or mine, but his spilled over into politically incorrect or what he considered harmless, lighthearted personal put-downs. Mine often tends to be a tad on the tasteless side—loathsome to one "fungus-faced toad-sucker" and apparently appealing to the next. To me, delivery fails if I alert the listener to a gag. Surprise is paramount, and the story must be weaved into plausible-sounding predicaments. The story progresses between reality and whopper.

We graduated a public affairs class every eight weeks when I taught journalism. We held a banquet six times a year. Each time, I invited a singing group of sunshine-faced young people from the mental institution in Indianapolis. The group sang their hearts out and became popular entertainment at dinners all over town. They ran into problems, however, when most of the performers became obese. The director had to limit their banquet food intake to a diet cola and apple. They even changed the name of the group to the Moron Tab 'n Apple Choir. That's how it works.

Wherever I've worked, students or co-workers would register the mild complaint that "Dave, we never know when you are serious."

It's a problem, especially in changing gears. One time I was introducing a true tragic topic for a feature writing class. A Canadian officer in the back of the room got the giggles. He thought my scenario was a "setup" for a punch line about to be delivered to an unsuspecting audience.

One student at the Defense Information School, in his course evaluation on my teaching performance in applied journalism, wrote, "Mr. Harris must be an outstanding instructor. I cannot relate to him." I fully understand the problem. I don't have much patience with someone who can play my role.

I don't always "wear well" with people. Most enjoy my company for a time. Then, they either become loyal friends or grow tired of the constant banter and move on. Fortunately, some rather hardy friends and co-workers stuck with me over decades. I just hope and pray it was they discovered some semblance of substance amidst the folly. I can put myself in the shoes of those who retreat from my companionship—I, too, tire quickly of someone who tells endless stories like me.

The writer of the book of Romans had insight about like-minded irritants, long before modern psychologists: *You, therefore, have no excuse, you who pass judgment on someone else, for at whatever point you judge the other, you are condemning yourself, because you who pass judgment do the same things.*

At first, hurt by abandonment or aloofness, I tried desperately to rescue the relationship. My success at this has been erratic. More recently, I have determined either there is a mutual bond and appreciation for a positive outlook on life, or perhaps I'm better off if a humorless compatriot finds friendship elsewhere—particularly if his or her outlook is dark and grim.

One delightful exception, a mix of the hilarious and gloomy, is my friend Gene Neudigate. He keeps me in stitches. One day he and I, en route to a men's retreat, stopped for a meal at Western Sizzlin', famous for their endless salad bar. Those were the days when I thought I could lose weight by eating salads—never mind that my platter was loaded with sunflower seeds, fatty salad dressing gluck and the works. Loading up for the third time, I sat down, satiated and content.

"Gene, when I eat, I feel close to God."

Full of half-feigned concern, he pointed at my heaping platter and scowled. "You oughta be," he retorted. "You're about to *die!*"

Gene, like me, sees humor in virtually any situation. Even so, he has a split personality. He's a lovable pessimist. No one pays any attention to his gloomy assessment of finances, politics and world affairs. If he complains about impending disaster, I am comforted, because I know by his expressing it that the calamity won't happen. I discovered over the years the odd secret to his happiness. Expecting the worst, he greets every new day pleasantly surprised. The failures and heartaches he just knew would come his way didn't materialize. Glory!

I think I finally figured out the reason for my excessive use of humor and lighthearted stories. As I grow older, I tell people, "Ever since I turned 57, I find that I have a story for every subject there is."

"Oh, isn't that nice," folks say politely, as they look around for the exit.

In earlier days, however, my use of humor became an attempt to distract people from my lack of academic depth. Or shall I say linear knowledge? What in the world is that? Here's a paradox. I have always been a slow reader—reading lines, linear. And yet, all my life I enjoyed writing. Go figure. Enlightenment came in the 1990s when I took the Meyers-Briggs assessment of my personality. I tested out as an "E-N-F-P," or someone who derives energy from others, rather than from within, and one who soaks up much of his information from intuition, feelings and perceptions, rather than books—I somehow capture data or insights out of the air.

I write news releases for scientists and engineers. Many times I have no idea what I'm talking about. I'll take the draft to a subject matter expert. Each time I think this person would give me a blank stare and say, "Dave, this makes utterly no sense. Why are you bringing me this drivel?" Amazingly it doesn't happen like that. Instead, the engineer will say, "Yeah! That pretty much captures it. Maybe change this word." He bought it! Another time, I wrote a skeleton briefing for our new Commander. He was to give this briefing to the Chief of Engineers in Washington, D.C. I asked for my boss' input. No response for weeks. I pressed him, because the presentation date was close. It was a weak briefing, I thought. Again, I had made it up out of the air. Finally, it was time for him to go to Washington. "This looks just fine," he said. "I'll use it just the way it is." I was shocked, but later, I got calls from all over the country asking for a copy. I guess the Chief liked it too.

An E-N-F-P often has the uncanny ability, seemingly, to read one's mind (though when I'm wrong, I'm spectacularly wrong). Oh, *now* they tell me about

Meyers-Briggs. This awareness would have come in handy starting in junior high. Rather than marry early, I would have understood the need to surround myself with a variety of people and not necessarily narrow my relationships down to an ill-fated marriage. And do I tire of people who act too much like me? "Don't hire another E-N-F-P like you," the Meyers-Briggs administrator advised. I do anyway. It increases the fun-quotient in the office—for me, anyway.

Having this personality would have explained how I successfully completed my undergraduate studies having read only one book, *The Adventures of Huckleberry Finn*, from cover to cover. Writing term papers about primarily that one book earned me some "A's." I demonstrated how "Jim," and not Huck, was the hero of the book. Mark Twain (Samuel Clemens) did not try to ridicule an African American. He illustrated the thoughtless abuse practiced by others toward slaves. Clemens himself paid the tuition for an African American to complete his college education. Those who call for the banning of this book from libraries are simply ill-informed.

Yet I, too, was ill-informed about Chaucer, Hegel, Mussolini, Kant, Einstein and Nietzsche—and humor became a smokescreen for my literary ignorance. My knowledge was limited to lighthearted bits and pieces, picked out of the air or etched in my brain from graffiti:

"God is dead."—Nietzsche

"Heh, heh."—God

Though I too often forget to "first assume positive intent" if I don't understand why someone exhibits somewhat strange behavior, the M-B instrument helps me, if I will stop to consider it, that there are different strokes for different folks. Sincere people respond because of varied work styles or personalities—slow, methodical and analytical, or possibly quick and driven. I may assign a story for the magazine. A writer takes two, three, four weeks to do it. Nuts! If I get tired of waiting, I'll do the story myself—in two hours or less. Even so, we need the producer, the analyst, the manager and the visionary—the accountant, engineer, pastor, laborer, general, puppeteer, story-teller, professor, homemaker, flautist, shortstop, kennel owner, caregiver, drill sergeant, undertaker and clown.

I suffered from mononucleosis in my final quarter at the University of Washington; yet, I needed to continue to graduation or face the draft and go to Vietnam as an infantryman. Too weak to read *Crime and Punishment*, I took my literature final based on a late-night movie rendition on the TV education channel.

I read more books in graduate school, studying mass communications at the University of Denver. My grades radically improved, but the subject matter suited me, and I took film arts and several other classes from 29-year-old Dr. Harry Spetnagel, who taught popular culture from 35mm slides of comic book covers.

The Meyers-Briggs, or similar profiles, can tend to typecast or pigeonhole someone—"Oh, I can't do that." Wrong. I may not be comfortable at some activity, but usually I can tough it out. I read what interests me and force myself to read the necessary-but-uninteresting. As for the mechanical, Dad was a mechanical and electrical genius. He invited me out on the job, but it was often too cold, too wet and too dark to appreciate, so I picked up none of it. Gene and I hit it off because we both have, as he describes it, "the mechanical ability of a walnut." Dad told me anything I couldn't eat, I broke—and vice versa. My mind knew what to avoid.

The E-N-F-P personality subconsciously finds its niche in the world. Admiring a dedicated math teacher, Howard Inouye, I thought I wanted to be an engineer or emulate him in teaching mathematics. I carried a "B" average throughout college freshman advanced algebra and trigonometry and calculus. In spring quarter, however, my intuition, perception and feelings told me to sign up for journalism class. I became sports editor for the Seattle Pacific College student newspaper, the *Falcon*. My E-N-F-P mind had no qualms about skipping many second quarter calculus classes to cover baseball games. I flunked calculus. I got an "A" in journalism. Wasted effort? No. My intuition knew what it was doing, even if my conscious mind did not. Having marginal grades in applying for graduate school, the university gave me "provisional" status pending outcome of my scores on the Graduate Record Examination. The results? "Your verbal scores are too low for admission to mass communications, but your *math* scores pulled you over the top, overall." Accepted. I finished grad school with a G.P.A. of 3.73, a respectable average, considering my head pulled off my matriculation and much of my piecemeal survival-level learning "out of the air."

Find out more about your own personality. Answer the questions at this website: **http://www.humanmetrics.com/cgi-win/JTypes2.asp**

Role Reversal?

Suzanne and I apparently don't communicate like other couples. She needs her space. I don't. Consequently, I constantly seek her opinion, her counsel, her companionship. Something's missing from my life when she's not around.

While some wives may seek out their husband's attention to discuss purchases, feelings and philosophical matters, in our marriage it is me who seeks my spouse's time and attention.

When I was going to graduate school in Denver, my former wife worked at Lowry Air Force Base. I sometimes had only one class a week and spent a lot of lonely time at home. I cleaned the house and fixed the meals. I even felt hurt if the family didn't care for my cooking or my housekeeping!

An enormous mutual respect flourishes my marriage today exceeding 26 years. Suzanne is a world-class mother and wife, full of wisdom and common sense. I couldn't have made a better choice.

A Life Utterly Transformed

Little did I know of the drama ahead when I first met the Kumps that sunny day in 1968 in California's San Joaquin Valley. Someone pretty as Michelle Pfeiffer in a red, white, blue checked maternity outfit stood at my Air Force duplex door. It was Shirley Kump, great with child, followed by, well, now he was known as J.B. Kump.

The two hailed from Missouri and J.B., as he insisted I call him, was newly assigned as a second lieutenant to our Castle Air Force Base Office of Information.

Johnnie Ben Kump, rather large for an Air Force officer, seemed out of character as the husband of such a stunning and charming blonde. But it wasn't long before I, too, discovered the charm that won his bride's heart.

As an only child, his mother called him Johnnie Ben. "What will my name be when I'm a grown up?" he asked one day when he was 9 years old and in the 4th grade.

"You'll always be Johnnie Ben," Mom replied, lovingly.

"That's not a big guy's name," he protested.

With a natural talent for art, Johnnie announced he wanted to be called "J.B." Sounded much more mature and distinguished, he thought (and a lot like one of his heroes, his grandfather "B.J."), and he spent hours writing his new nickname. An admirer of Walt Disney, he copied his hero and made circles instead of periods in his signature.

Several years later at camp, he scribbled his new "grown up" name and last name on a roster at scout camp registration, circles and all. After awhile that first day he was horrified to hear a most embarrassing announcement over the public address system. "Will...JoBo Rump...please come to the administration building?" Some 25 years went by before I was able to prod him to screw up enough courage to tell the story publicly as he had told it privately to a few close loved ones. That's how I knew he regarded me as a special friend.

As an aside, I must mention here another name story. Young people torment their fellows over names, and it wasn't until I was in the Air Force teaching journalism that I fully understood the sensitivity and importance of getting one's name right. At the Defense Information School, where both J.B. and I taught some 10 years after we met, we had a saying, "Misspell the General's name and your knickers will be aflame."

As a Boy Scout I attended a weekend camp at Fort Lawton in Seattle. The Scout Master told us to handwrite our last name and then our first name. He then appointed a scout to type up the roster, after which he called roll. My bunk mate, Brian Baird, and I listened for our names.

"Bird...Brain? Is there someone here named Bird Brain?"

Those old Underwoods didn't have spell check. Today, Washington State has a U.S. Congressman named Brian Baird. I wonder if it's the same guy!

I guess you could call me a "Closet Christian" in those early days in the Air Force. J.B. and I became good friends, but if he and I had been taken to court for being a Christian, I'm sure there would not be enough evidence to convict us. Oh, we were faithful to our wives and devoted family men, but our traded banter and language would certainly not cause a sinner to seek us out as someone who could lead him to an assurance of salvation.

I had prayed when I knew I would take over as Chief of the office and when I was awaiting the new second lieutenant. I felt inadequate, shy and insecure—rather intimidated by the protocol and authority of not only high-ranking officers, but squared-away peers, as well. Though I prayed for someone compatible to work with, my faith was weak, and I fully expected my Assistant Chief to be arrogant, confident and far more competent than I.

Our first visit put me at ease. But J.B. totally won our hearts a day or two later when he invited my family, including 1-year-old Gary, to their temporary quarters for dinner. As soon as we entered, J.B. punched up a reel-to-reel tape recording that he had made. "Hello, Pluto!" J.B.'s squeaky-voiced Disney characterization became his trademark. The tape went on for perhaps 30 minutes, intending to delight Gary with stories and cartoon character impressions. But I was the one who was most enthralled, relaxed and relieved. J.B. was sent from God, someone whose personality, foibles and humor fit me and what I needed like a glove.

Barbara and I, Shirley and J.B. spent nearly every weekend together, making chip dip and home movies, sharing laughs and silly songs. What a release from the tensions of the daily grind of media relations and Broken Arrow nuclear accident drills. I eagerly looked forward to our regular gatherings.

Though we served together only eight months or so in that first assignment, our paths crossed several times in and after the Air Force. I needed his counsel most at DINFOS—the Defense Information School—during a crisis time in my life (my second divorce) but not before J.B. faced the greatest crisis in his life.

I learned of the miraculous outcome of his crisis over a meal in Indianapolis when he first reported to DINFOS at Fort Benjamin Harrison. I had heard that my friend, unbelievably, had spent two months in an Air Force mental hospital at Sheppard Air Force Base, Texas. How could it be? No one was more vibrant or mentally alive than J.B. There must be some mistake. Surely someone had gotten the story screwed up.

I had been attending a small Nazarene church in Indianapolis and grew closer to the Lord as I attended every service. Susan, my second wife, had taken sick one Sunday. We had attended a fairly large Baptist church down the street, but it was so "programmed," we never met the pastor! Longing for more interaction, I wandered that Sunday into Fall Creek Church of the Nazarene. A recent change of pastors resulted in a dwindling congregation and, though someone played the piano, a beautiful organ sat silent through the song service. John Payton, an elder, asked me after the service, "Does your wife play the organ?"

"No, but I do."

John marched me up to the lovely organ, and I sat down and began to play some hymns. John's wife, Henrietta, made a bee-line to the organ, tears streaming down her face.

"You don't know how long and hard we've prayed for someone like you to come and play the organ!"

How could I back out of that appeal? Soon they had me teaching Sunday School and some of the Wednesday night services. I thought it was important to brush up a bit on the faith of my fathers so that I could teach and play from the heart.

J.B. came to town shortly after that, fully recovered from his psychotic episode, having served a tour in the Philippines after his recovery and having inquired of me whether there was a "slot" at DINFOS for an instructor. I was thrilled we'd be serving again.

Susan and I had him over for dinner. But, sheepishly thinking I didn't want to embarrass him, I skipped saying the blessing over the food as I had become accustomed. Even though we had not seen each other for the better part of 10 years, our conversation resumed as if we had never separated. I was reluctant, however, to push the issue of the mental illness. I was curious, but the subject would come up in due time.

A week or two later, Shirley and his children, John and Linda, joined him. Again in temporary quarters, he invited Susan and me over for dinner. It was my time to be embarrassed. Here was this man I had known for his salty and spicy stories, some of which mocked ministers, and who had shown no interest in spiritual things. But at the table, his large hands grabbed the hands of his wife and daughter (we quickly clasped hands as well) and, he said with a sincere and booming voice, "Our precious Heavenly Father, we thank you for this glorious day and for traveling mercies and for these precious loved ones. Thank you for this food and bless the hands that prepared it. In the Name of our Lord, Amen." I couldn't believe my ears. Something or someone had come over my friend and radically changed his life. After a few weeks, the time was right to share his story with me.

"I was attending the Air Force Short Course in Public Communication at the University of Oklahoma," he began. "I was lonesome for Shirley one Saturday night, and I had bronchitis. My classmates all wanted to go to town to party. I just decided to stay in my room, but first I thought I'd walk over to the university clinic to see if they had something for my bronchitis.

"They told me I was in luck. They had a drug they'd give me for the bronchitis. I swallowed the pills with some water and intended to go straight to bed but a roommate convinced me to join him in a beer—that combination was to cause me some serious problems. Soon I was dreaming. I dreamt I was fully aware that I was dreaming and that I was walking around campus in my underwear. 'Wow! I sure couldn't get away with this in real life. Only in my dream!' Then the campus police found me found wandering around on campus in my underwear," he recalled.

"The next thing I knew I was dreaming that I was riding in an ambulance in a straightjacket. 'This dream seemed so real,' I thought."

It was.

The combination of the medicine and the alcohol had triggered a psychotic episode and soon he found himself as a patient in the psychiatric ward of an Air Force mental hospital.

"I was sure the staff was trying to kill me," he said. "I slid my pancakes into a magazine by my side, because I didn't want them to poison me."

One day J.B., alarmed, went up to the front of a television set. He thought he saw the hospital staff on the screen.

"OK! I know who you are. I know what you're trying to do. You're spying on me."

For much of this time, Shirley was following the situation and getting reports while staying with her parents and the couple's two children in Missouri. Such unexpected behavior was almost more than she could bear. Confused and bewildered, she even questioned her love for her husband. How would she cope with a virtual stranger whom she had loved so dearly when he was in his right mind? And how would she raise their two children? After all, the doctors had told her her husband would probably never be well enough again to earn a living.

She determined to settle it. She traveled to the hospital and got to visit with J.B.

"I knew right then I still loved him, and we would get through this together."

After weeks of therapy in the hospital, J.B. still felt paranoid and rather helpless. He wandered the halls to pass the time and to think—could he begin to make sense of all that had happened to him? One day he happened to stop by the little hospital chapel. He sat down and picked up some literature by Dr. Norman Vincent Peale, including *Guideposts* magazine. Reading the material, J.B. began to think about God and to pray that God would deliver him.

God answered his halting prayer. Every day J.B. made more progress. His thinking cleared. He felt more and more confident. As he improved, his faith and his prayer life picked up strength.

It wasn't long before Captain Johnnie B. Kump went home to the loving arms of Shirley and his children, as well as his mother and in-laws.

The story doesn't end there, of course. It was customary for a psychotic episode to essentially end the career of an Air Force officer. How could he be trusted to lead during the stressful times of war and peace? That's where the miracle begins. J.B. served with distinction in the Philippines, involved with Operation Baby Lift, transporting Vietnam orphans to the United States. He was by far the most effective and popular instructor at the Defense Information School. His interest in counseling and drama served him well there. He volunteered to play roles of numerous staff officers during joint staff exercises with the students. He added a unique voice and accent for each role, and a half-dozen fellow instructors would peer over his cubicle to observe the natural entertainer as he delighted the students with his renditions.

But God knew to send J.B. my way at the right time. Facing a second divorce crushed my spirit. I felt devastated. J.B. would walk me to a classroom nearly every morning with a listening ear and wise counsel acquired during some dark days of his own. His friendship and godly cheer was just what the doctor ordered. I dated a Christian Army reservist named Frances. "Maybe God has someone else for you," he'd say. I then dated Debbie, who was active in Gospel music. Someone so compatible with me. "Maybe God has someone else for you," J.B. repeated. About the time I gave up, Suzanne walked into my life and sat down in the back of Fall Creek Church. This time, J.B. gave me no warning. He seemed to know Mrs. Right had arrived.

Rather than ending his career after recovery from mental illness, J.B. was promoted twice more—to lieutenant colonel. I, myself, was passed over for promotion during a surplus of leftover Vietnam captains, and I left as a captain after 12 years of active duty. Not J.B. He went on to two prominent assignments in Germany and retired from the Space Command in California. All the while, he was active in the Officers Christian Fellowship. He became an elder in his church. And he was hired by Lockheed to serve as media relations chief for the Space Shuttle program at Kennedy Space Center. My only regret is that I never visited J.B. at Cape Canaveral during the awesome launch of one of those big birds. Maybe someday. Between stints serving as District Director and Press Secretary for a Congressman in Florida, J.B. worked for Boeing an then, longing for more active ministry, he served SAT-7, a Christian organization that broadcasts the gospel message into the Middle East and Northern Africa.

Talk is cheap. There are those who can say all the right words about finding, knowing and serving God. I've read solid, well-researched books by Charles Colson and Lee Strobel about the scientific, prophetic and historical evidence for a personal, loving and just God. But there is no greater evidence than a transformed life. To me, there is no more vivid transformation than God's handiwork in the life of my dear buddy, J.B. Kump.

Head and Shoulders,
Knees and Toes

I've forgotten her name, but the perky young lady was one of my most memorable students at the Defense Information School. But if she was memorable, why did I forget her most useful lesson?

I love it when I can learn from one of my students. She said she had studied drama and liked to help out around the stage. I had struggled with tangled extension cords, and she showed me a way to wind the wire to avoid tangles. It was brilliant. It would have made the rest of my days so much easier. Such a practical lesson. Life-changing.

The day she graduated, I forgot.

I thought of some captivating chapters for this book, as well.

Vanished.

One night I dreamed of an air-tight business plan to make a million dollars. I got so excited I awoke. Should I get up and write it down? No need. This idea would turn the world upside down. I feared I would not be able to sleep, much less forget this incredible brainchild by morning. I slept. I forgot.

Even so, What's-her-name, my vivacious student, was unforgettable. Not, sadly, for her extension-coiling technique, but for her musical drama.

She told of her talented drama teacher who encouraged his young high school pupils to lose their inhibitions by singing and acting out the song, *Head and shoulders, knees and toes*. Good idea! I thought that was the end of the story. Far from it.

Her class's next assignment was to learn to sing the song backward. No big deal. Or was it? Each student had to sing it in such a way that it could be recorded, and then played in reverse and sound normal and understandable.

Nice story. But then she floored me by performing the song backward on the spot—as if you had heard a phonograph record or tape played backward:

It sounded like a tone-deaf Russian singing in the shower:

"Seot dna seenk, seot dna seenk, sredluohs dna daeh!"

Never again have I seen such towering genius. Shaken, my life will never be the same.

Don't Date Someone with a Funny Name

My Sunday School teachers gave me some good advice, not always followed: Don't date anyone I know could not someday be my spouse.

I have a corollary: Be careful about marrying someone that could get you stuck with a silly combination of names. For instance, Snoop Doggy Dog should not marry Winnie the Pooh. Go figure.

In our church in Indiana, the youth pastor and his wife, Doug and Sandy Ehrgott, had a lovely daughter named Beverly. Suzanne, of course, has a nursery rhyme or song for every one of life's situations, and so does Beverly. One day Beverly's parents sat her down to tell her she was going to have a new baby brother or sister. They had nicknamed Beverly "Boo-Boo." With careful sensitivity, Doug and Sandy explained to Boo-Boo the delights of a new arrival in their family.

Recalling her pre-school poetry, Boo-Boo pointed repeatedly at her Mommy and Daddy saying, "That's what you get for jumping on the bed!"

The biggest fear in our circle of friends was that someday Boo-Boo might marry our buddy's son Matt. Nothing wrong with Matt, except for his last name—Ballou.

She'd never hear the end of it—Boo-Boo Ballou.

Recently I heard from Boo-Boo's Daddy that she had grown up, married (not Matt) and just had a baby, Ruth. Grandpa calls her Boo-Boo-Roo.

And my buddy Jack Barron wrote to say that his daughter, whom we nicknamed Sherri Berri, married a guy named Brian Perry. Hey, Jack! It could be a lot worse!

Presidential Pushers and a 5-Star Bathroom User

When the Air Force wanted to appoint me as liaison officer to the Defense Information School, they sent me to the Pentagon for an orientation.

My host took me to see a lieutenant colonel in the media relations division. The officer told me that at 2:30 a.m. a White House official had awakened him to tell him two Air Force technical sergeants, stewards on Jimmy Carter's Air Force One, had been arrested for selling marijuana.

"I sat on the edge of the bed in my underwear," he said. "I asked myself, 'Now what do I do? I hope nobody calls me!'"

It was a comforting visit. I think the very same things every time the Air Force called me with bad news at 2:30 in the morning.

Later, I had to use the bathroom. The Pentagon is a maze of corridors, and it's easy to get lost. The historic building houses ornate offices of the Secretary of Defense, the Joint Chiefs of Staff and many luminaries. I just couldn't find a bathroom, so I asked an Air Force sergeant to show me where one was.

"Have I got a deal for you, Captain!"

Good grief. What now?

He took me down a fancy hall. There were the palatial offices of General Omar Bradley, legendary World War II hero who was still alive and enjoyed access to his Pentagon offices for life.

"General Omar Bradley likely won't be in today," he said confidently. "You can use his private bathroom."

I did, with great reverence and awe.

Bulb Sales Genius

Gene Neudigate made a living for 40-plus years selling the most expensive light bulbs you could find—General Electric. When a customer called asking if he sold a less expensive brand, his standard reply was, "We don't sell junk."

Jokingly he called himself the Illumination-Transportation Consultant. For years he delivered bulbs out of a truck. Strolling through a mall or a restaurant, he constantly looks up at the lighting and says, "That's an 65R30FL." It's a wild experience going into a grocery store with him. Try as he might, he just can't resist walking up to the light bulb display. He's all retail. "Look at this mess," he grumbles. "Bulbs are a money-loser for this store because of the way they are displayed." He'll give you a lecture on just where each bulb should perch on the shelf for optimum sales placement. Sometimes he just can't stand it anymore, and he'll start shuffling the bulbs.

I'll ask, "Is this one of your customers?"

"Good heavens, no," he replies in horror. "If it were my customer, the display would look nothing like this!"

I admire Gene's mastery of light bulbs. It amazes me how he can get people to buy the most expensive product just by rearranging the shelves. I remember when Dad bought me some wholesale bulbs when I was 13. I went door to door with a raggedy brown jacket, carrying the bulbs in a torn, wrinkled shopping bag. I could never understand why a sale was a rarity.

Gene turned on the bulb in my head. Oh, to be 13 again. Retail! Display! With what the Illumination-Transportation Consultant taught me, I think I could sell a million of them. Well, I could unload my last three 60-watt four-packs anyway.

I'll bet you anything.

International Diversity

I was glad that Suzanne could go with me when I flew to El Paso to conduct a newspaper seminar at Fort Bliss. We sampled Mexican food at a few places in El Paso, but Juarez, Mexico, was just over the border, and we wanted to taste some totally authentic Mexican cuisine.

Our soldier host was gracious enough to loan us a car to drive into Juarez. We asked him where the best Mexican food was over there.

"It doesn't exist in Juarez," he said. "But they have great Chinese food."

OK, OK. We enjoyed some tasty egg rolls, fried rice, almond chicken and sweet and sour pork in Juarez.

Shucks. We had to look for some authentic Mexican food stateside. The meals in El Paso were delicious, but they seemed too Americanized.

We drove west—maybe as far as New Mexico. We saw a sign that the next town was featured in *Life* magazine for its world famous Mexican food.

Anxiously, we drove directly to this renowned restaurant.

Back in Indianapolis, we were used to "Gringos," where we got their $2.99 platter.

Now, we eagerly devoured everything on our plates at this highly touted eatery.

Authentic. Lovingly prepared.

Tastefully appointed.

Disappointed.

We were two hicks longing for Gringo's back home.

Celestial Guidance Just in Time

How do we know our calling? I've learned over the years through readings and seeking that one discovers the will of God by a number of means. Most of us don't get the blinding light or thunderous voice from heaven. I've often thought that if an angel appeared in my bedroom it would startle the p-jeebies out of me. Most of us find out God's will for our lives through rather ordinary means: reading scripture (God's will won't contradict his Word), our personality type, gifts, natural tendencies, counsel and, perhaps the last way, is circumstances—knocking on doors to see which open and close. People tend to try the last method first, but that can get us into trouble.

I read a story of a young woman who felt called to minister to disadvantaged youth. She made an appointment with her pastor for guidance. He said, "This is delightful. I just received a letter from a Christian organization in Rhode Island, and your background and calling would make a perfect match." Her response: "Oh, I don't think so. Do you know of anything closer to home?"…Whatever happened to "I'll go where You want me to go"?

In my own case, I took Bill Gothard's test for spiritual gifts. I thought I should be a teacher, but the test indicated I lacked academic depth and love of research. No, the test indicated I am an exhorter—inciting one to a decision or action through advice or, as Webster says, argument (each gift comes with its potential downside)! I toyed with the idea of a second master's degree in counseling, but the curriculum methods of measurement and grading (not necessarily the content) discouraged and frustrated me. Then, too, I met and heard about many folks with problems I simply felt inadequate to remedy. My co-workers will tell you, however, I offer no end of advice, often about inconsequential matters!

One of the most vivid tests of my calling and God's will, perhaps, involved whether I should continue with the Air Force after 12 years or get out. I was one of the "Vietnam Hump," a glut of captains who remained in the Air Force after the war. My personality and gifts were not well suited for barking out orders in combat. I knew that. However, I had discovered an approach to emergencies that eventually served me well. I learned the hard way. I have had to cover as many as a dozen fatal aircraft accidents, attending to media relations. My experienced boss

was out of town the first time it happened, although I had participated in a number of accident response exercises. When the real thing first happened, I was frantic. The required access to the commander vanished and I needed his approval in
order to release information. I winged it, and probably made every mistake and
uttered everything to the press that I shouldn't have. Later, higher headquarters
questioned some of my decisions and asked for a report. Fortunately my gift of
word weaseling kept me from serious trouble.

I learned from that incident, fortunately. In a few months I faced another accident. I remembered how ineffective I was in my previous frantic state. This time
I determined to maintain my composure. If something fell through the cracks, so
be it. My words and actions would not impact life or limb. During the ordeal, an
airman asked me, "Lieutenant Harris, how can you remain so calm at a time like
this?" It was music to my ears. The other way didn't work. Since then, I remembered those words, and managed to take the calming approach in most situations.
It works far better than losing one's self-control.

Before I found out I was not suited to be an in-depth teacher, I sought and
received an assignment that I enjoyed immensely as an Air Force journalism
instructor at the Defense Information School, Fort Benjamin Harrison, Indiana.
I suppose my affinity for writing and interest in journalism helped make up for
lack of academic profundity. The course was eight weeks long, covering short
exposures to various journalistic styles and approaches. I collected and told
numerous lighthearted stories and perfected their timing. I had found my niche.
My evaluations by students were high—as long as I wasn't too academically
demanding of my class. I tried to make it fun, tossing Tootsie Roll Pops in class
when students were scheduled for my session after lunch following a tough exam.
More about that in the next chapter.

At the 12-year point in my career, I faced a critical promotion point. It was
"up or out." If the promotion board didn't select me for major, I would have to
consider separating from the Air Force. It was a choice, but the Air Force would
strongly influence that choice by their selection.

Technical Sergeant Charlie Price, a fun-loving African American, had a grim
look on his face and motioned to have a private word from me. I excused myself
from a student conference. "Captain, I didn't see your name on the list," he told
me. I had been passed over for promotion. My heart sank. Now what? The Air
Force offered me two options: accept $15,000 severance pay, or stay for a second
promotion consideration coming up in a year. Chances for promotion as a result
of a second consideration were less than the first go-round, but my employment
options were few. I looked into some Civil Service opportunities, but several

doors closed. One day a fellow instructor, a civilian, said he was leaving and suggested I look into the vacancy. I would love that job, essentially identical to my Air Force teaching position. I applied but made no progress. The process was anything but encouraging.

It was decision time. The Pentagon wanted to know if I would leave or stay for one more year. They needed my signed paperwork by the following Monday if I wanted to stay. Meanwhile, I learned that I could improve my chances for the Civil Service job if I talked my boss into submitting a by-name request and if I put on my application, "Within 120 days of military separation." Suzanne and I drove to Chicago to hand-deliver the application one week before the Air Force deadline. I prayed, "Lord, show me your will before I must mail my decision." The drop-dead mailing time was 10 a.m. Friday. I called Chicago on Tuesday. "Did you process my application?" They hadn't gotten to it. I called Wednesday. No progress. Thursday. "We have processed your application, but there are a number of other qualified applicants."

A day before mail drop time and no confirmation. That's it. God must want me to stay in the Air Force one more year. I signed the paperwork and dropped it into Thursday's mail pick-up. Decision made.

Friday morning at 9 a.m., Chicago called. "Captain Harris, your Civil Service application met all the requirements for the instructor position, and you were the only one on the list." My clear, unmistakable answer? It suddenly dawned on me. I had asked God for guidance on my decision before the mailing deadline. He had given me the answer just one hour sooner than the 10 a.m. Friday pick-up. That's it! I called Suzanne, and then the Pentagon. "Monday you'll be getting my paperwork to stay in the Air Force. Tear it up!!!" A woman captain's soothing voice was on the other end of the line. "I understand. Don't worry. I'll intercept it for you."

I had jumped the gun by 24 hours. But 24 years later I know God's decision was best. I joined the reserve, earned two more promotions and a reserve pension that kicks in at age 60, and I completed a fulfilling Civil Service career in Indianapolis, Heidelberg and Seattle, a career that offers its own pension, a blessing I'm already enjoying.

Certainly, God reveals His will…just in time.

Memorable Speakers Found
the Key to My Mind

I can think of a number of great speakers over the years, but maybe most weren't all that good. I can remember the speaker, but not what he said in many cases. Three of them, however, grabbed and kept my attention, and I remember much of what they said.

The best of the three I'll call Hank. He spoke to the Defense Information School, and he was some kind of globe-hopping goodwill ambassador from the State Department. As we entered the auditorium, the stage and walls were decorated with all manner of cultural finery. Hank greeted us in several languages and threw candy and bottles of beverages at us. Throughout his presentation he was most animated and kept throwing goodies from all over the world. He wanted to plant an appreciation for people of other cultures, and he was most effective. It was upon seeing him that I would throw Tootsie Roll Pops at my students after they had been up half the night studying for a morning test, only to drag into my class after lunch. You can't fall asleep when people keep throwing candy at you.

The second speaker, Professor Ed, spoke with similar energy, even though he was getting on in years. He taught on newspaper design and layout. He didn't need a lot of props. I recall his use of the pregnant pause—much like Paul Harvey. Once he abruptly stopped talking and looked over to the corner of the room. After about 10 seconds, he pointed to the object of his peering. I craned my neck to see what caught his eye. It turned out to be nothing. It was a simple and memorable lesson about eye flow. From then on, I followed his lead in teaching my students that everything they put on a newspaper page must consider how it attracted and moved the eye to the desired entry point, sweep direction and exit. The eye first found the photos and graphics and then went to the headline. You didn't want to design a page so the eye first sees a picture toward the middle of the page and then is expected to go back up to the top. Eye flow is like gravity. See? I remembered most of what Professor Ed said.

The third speaker is an expert in church growth. I'll call him Pastor Pete. He said to keep the attention of a Sunday School class, you have to plan something unusual and seemingly out of place during the class session. He had asked for commitment from each class member for a 13-week series, but then he himself was called out of town. He chose a knowledgeable but rather dull teacher, Ruben, to take his place.

"Just plan something unusual and out of the ordinary to capture their attention," he advised his replacement.

Upon his return to the church two weeks later, the place was abuzz with the fascinating class session taught by Ruben, the dull substitute. Pastor Pete sought him out and asked him what he had done.

"I brought a big, beautiful, red delicious apple, wrapped in tissue, and gave it to a lady. I told her it was freshly washed and would she take a bite of it? She smiled and took a bite. I looked at the class, pointed at her accusingly and shouted, 'That's how it all started!' And I began teaching about sin."

Later, Jim Owens, who had heard Pastor Pete's story the same time I did, team-taught a class with me about contemporary issues. He'd take one side and I the other, and we'd debate the week's topic. One particular week the topic was gun control. Remembering Pastor Pete's advice for something out of the ordinary, Jim was ready. I gave my side of the argument. When it was Jim's turn, he pulled out an ominous-looking deadly black revolver and placed it deliberately on the table. Everyone listened intently. He won the debate.

That week we had an extra visitor, Pastor Tom. Apparently Jim had mentioned the revolver beforehand, and Tom showed up in a kind of security role. He liked the idea of something unusual and out of the ordinary, and he was there to make sure the attention step wouldn't be the talk of the town for years to come.

Boot 'Em Up to Heaven with Safe Sects

Quite by accident I became involved with the early use of the Internet around 1980 at the Defense Information School. They bought into a computer-assisted instructional system that spanned the nation. I got hooked on electronic discussion bulletin boards on theology. Wow! Folks had some weird ideas, and their disbelief of traditional Christianity almost always fell into one or more reasons scripture gives for such rejection: ignorance, pride or moral failure. I later dialogued on a system called GEnie, mostly comparing traditional, orthodox Christianity with Latter Day Saints.

With people who followed various cults and sects, I tried to point out how they conflicted with historical proofs and precepts of the Bible—how in every case a cult promoted self-deification or venerated a mere human rather than the God-Man, Jesus Christ.

I contemplated writing a book about the in-roads I attempted to make with the cultists in a book called *Boot 'em up to heaven,* alluding to the computer discussions I had with unbelievers. Unbelievers? That in itself is a misleading term. Everyone has a belief system, and often one can find a flaw in it. When folks would ask me why I was so sure my religion was correct, I used two points: my faith is not a religion—monotonous repetition, as doing something "religiously"—my faith is a relationship with a personal God who cares about every aspect of my life. Secondly, it's not something I made up; it is plainly outlined in God's Word.

But why do I accept the Bible as God's Word if mere men wrote it? Too much archaeological, scientific and prophetic evidence makes it impossible to find otherwise if one is a sincere seeker. Diverse men—shepherds, tax collectors and kings—could not attain such thematic unity without supernatural inspiration from God. Lawyers and scientists, having tried to discredit the Bible, ended up as believers.

Then I thought of another title, *Safe Sects.* What if one found confidence in the reality of the God of the Bible but became confused as to which denomination to pursue? I attempted to think through the safest route. Was there controversy, for example, on mode of baptism? Immersion was a safe, inclusive choice. I hear folks refusing to investigate God's companionship, citing diversity of denominations as a reason to reject Him. Nuts. I have found a common spirit among many denominations in worshiping all over the world. The comforting thing in the many styles offered in differing denominations is that the head of the churches is not, as I said, a celebrated man of letters. No, Jesus Christ is the only Head we need.

But so many topics I could cover in such a book involved ritual or behavioral options. No one could earn his way to heaven, and so the common denominator must be a seeking, loving heart that experiences sorrow for one's God-rejecting attitudes and actions, turns from one's rebellion and invites the Savior into his life, trusting Him, seeking His daily companionship, along with fellow believers, and divine guidance. Dallas Willard's *Divine Conspiracy* paints such an indescribably rich and exhilarating, adventuresome picture of this blissful state of sonship with God. Honestly considered, it is a relationship far too powerful, appealing, captivating and freeing to ignore. The closer one gets to God, the less one need worry about unsafe sects. Your nose knows. It's like walking into the wrong house.

Immediately and instinctively you know when you're not safe at home.

Soccer Kick Boots 'Em Through the Uprights

For the most part, I have been particularly blessed with in-laws. My sister Laurie's husband, John Wesley Johnson, was one of four children of Warren and Jean, who were missionaries in South Africa. Warren will tell you of frightening adventures in South Africa. Among his stories are his encounters with deadly mamba snakes. Around the fields you could spot a number of anti-venom stations. Bitten by a mamba, you wouldn't survive unless you took the anti-venom within 20 minutes.

John never worried about snakes much. He was an adventurous MK—missionary's kid. Now an attorney, he marvels that he is still alive after his carefree days in Africa. He is still full of energy, involved from Poulsbo, Washington, in a mind-spinning number of land and business development, assisted living, legal, civic, international Christian outreach projects and family activities. He and Laurie find themselves scurrying from one of their child's soccer games to another.

John played soccer as a boy in South Africa. A fellow MK—Gary Anderson—regularly played on the same field. They were good friends. Years later, both young men returned to the States to complete their education. John ultimately decided he wanted to go to law school in Philadelphia. Gary went to Syracuse University. By then an accomplished soccer and rugby player, he was persuaded to try out on the football team as a kicker. He excelled. Upon graduation, this former missionary soccer player was drafted into the National Football League. One day, John called me and said he had tickets to the Seahawks game with the Philadelphia Eagles. He told me the story of his pal, Gary, and said he and several male members of his family were going to see Gary kick for the Eagles. Would I like to come along? Of course!

We enjoyed watching Gary play. After the game we stood at the entrance where the players would come out, sign autographs and head for the bus to the airport. John had pre-arranged to have Gary talk with us. I had thought, "What an easy job—he has to work about two minutes a week!" Gary was not a large player. He told about how sometimes he was the only one between the opposing ball carrier with behemoth blockers and the goal post. I can just imagine myself in such a predicament. C-R-R-U-N-CH!!

Gary played for a number of pro football teams. Like the story of the tortoise and the hare, Gary just kept kicking—1 point here, 3 points there. Not a huge tally, but sometimes a point or two could make the difference between victory and defeat.

Gary enjoyed a wonderful opportunity to play in the Big Leagues. My assessment was that he was in a support role, like that of a lineman—not a star but, nonetheless, an essential part of the team.

Support role? I was wrong. Now here's a life lesson for those of us who think our small contributions don't make that much difference. Gary Anderson proved otherwise; John's school-days soccer buddy consistently kicked those "insignificant" little 1- and 3-pointers all the way into the record books.

Gary went on to achieve the distinction as the NFL's all-time highest scorer.

The Missing Gas Cap Key

Dallas and Millie Lynch delighted me with their homespun Kentucky-Indiana language and stories. I stayed with the husband-wife insurance team during bachelor days.

Dallas murdered the Queen's English with his third-grade-level speech. Successful as an insurance man, he and Millie traveled around the country. His recollection: "We saw some baboon trees on our trip to Gethsemane National Park after we crossed the Mohammed Desert." His word for "snorkeling" was "snuggling." A bird big enough for you to ride on was an "ostachuck." Millie, Suzanne and Tami, all of whom worked in the agency, would laugh until tears rolled down their cheeks.

Dallas and Millie faithfully attended Fall Creek Church of the Nazarene. Millie would greet the children, telling each one how nice he looked or how sweet she smelled. One Sunday she missed greeting a small boy. He would not be ignored.

"'Mell me, Miwwie!"

Millie was to drive herself to visit a relative two states away. After she departed, Dallas noticed with alarm she had forgotten the key to the gas cap. Millie, of course, discovered her problem the first time she stopped for gas. Concerned, she told the attendant.

"Not to worry," he said. "This key ring has a hundred of them. One of them's bound to fit."

After a long delay, they concluded that none they tried would work.

A stranger, observing the failed attempt, offered to try his. It worked!

Millie quickly shoved the nozzle into the receptacle and turned around to thank the stranger.

He was nowhere to be found—not a trace.

Had Millie encountered an angel, unaware?

84

The Pope and Me

I was most privileged to serve in the Air Force Reserve, which deployed me to Verona, Italy, and Germany.

In Verona we stayed at a nice hotel downtown; we ate at the Italian air base. I noticed they served us pork that was quite pink in the middle. Concerned, I checked with "Doc," who deployed with us. Doc was a veterinarian. The Air Force assigns veterinarians to check the quality of food that airmen eat. Often you will find them inspecting raw meat in commissaries. Doc reassured us that the pink pork had been cooked to the required 180 degrees temperature.

Buddy J.B. Kump had arranged for me to do a base newspaper evaluation in Germany following my two-week tour in Verona. The Air Force travel office gave me a train ticket to Rome, where I was to have a 36-hour layover, and then fly on Ethiopian Airlines to Germany.

I was interested in seeing the art and pageantry at the Vatican, and the travel office folks told me the Rome USO was just down the street from there. They also warned me not to take a Roman taxi—the USO was within walking distance from the train station.

I rode all night on the crowded train. I had to wait several hours to find a seat. When I did, I sat next to an Italian who was eating some kind of pungent sausage. I could barely breathe.

Arriving in Rome late on a hot Saturday morning, I grabbed my two suitcases and tried to walk in the direction of the USO. Wearing my Air Force blues, I sweated profusely. After half an hour I was lost and exhausted. I decided to pay any price to get a taxi. The cab drove me two more blocks to the USO! By wasting time walking, I missed the daily tour to the Vatican down the street. I was to visit the hallowed halls on my own.

I knew I had time to attempt a view of the Pope greeting the people from his window Sunday, but I was told I may not have that opportunity. The Pope had scheduled a beatification Mass and may not go to his window. I thought I'd try Sunday morning to go to the Mass in St. Peter's Basilica. When I got there, I found long lines of people. I learned I needed a special invitation to get in. Just then a woman came out of a side door and asked in English, "Would anyone like a special invitation to the Mass?" I got one.

With my invitation in hand, I was whisked inside, around to the back of the altar, to one of the best seats in the house. I watched the Pope celebrate under dozens of TV lights, and during a lull in the proceedings, I saw a chance to slip out—I wanted to get a good spot under the Pope's window just in case he appeared there.

I was overwhelmed at what I saw outside. I was inside a roped-off area and beyond the ropes were perhaps 100,000 people or more. I turned around and looked up to find the famous window. I was standing directly under the balcony—if the Pope showed up, I likely would not see a thing. I stood there just in case.

Sure enough, he appeared. I could barely see the top of his cap. I reached for my camera and discovered I had only two pictures left on the roll. So, grabbing the opportunity, I took two pictures of the little white cap. End of the roll.

A minute or two later, the Pope was finishing his greeting. With no more film, I watched, wide-eyed, as the Pope leaned out from the balcony, looked straight down at me, and waved.

I don't understand Italian or Latin, but I'm convinced of what he said to conclude his remarks.

"Hi, Dave!"

Tayk Nauwtice

Despite at least two speed-reading courses, I'm a painfully slow reader. Problem is I want to slow down and live the story. When it's textbook material, I go even slower, but I retain much of what I read—less so as I grow older.

Andy Rooney once said that someone wanted him to read a book about Islam. He showed off his library and said he loved his books and knew them well. His brain was full of what his books taught him. In order to put another book in his head, he said he'd have to remove one of his beloved volumes from his brain to make room. That's why young people are so good at computers, he asserted. "They're empty-headed."

During my stay in Heidelberg, I wasn't able to attend Air Force Reserve unit weekend duties, so I took long, boring correspondence courses to maintain my status and earn points toward retirement.

One course had books made up of 3,500 pages of required reading material. My co-worker, Staff Sergeant George Whitley, said he read textbooks during commercials while watching TV.

I remembered the advice of two of my King's High School teachers. "Make use of your minutes," Mr. Thiessen reminded us often. If we were 3 minutes early to class, open a book and read a page or two to get a leg up on homework. I don't recall that we ever heeded that advice in high school. We were too busy trying to outdo each other with the give and take of clever conversation.

"Take notes and take notice of your notes," Dr. Lush admonished in his Australian accent. We tried to emulate his diction, but it wasn't until years later that I followed either of my teachers' advice.

I remembered what they said after I dozed off with that correspondence course in Germany. I calculated the weeks available for completion of the course and found that I needed to read 20 pages a day—10 pages walking to work and 10 pages walking home—a cinch!

I'd have never made it though college, graduate school or those awful Air Force courses had not those once irritating high school instructions ingrained themselves in my 16-year-old brain so long ago.

"Make use of your minutes!" Thank you, Mr. Thiessen.

"Tayk nauwts, and tayk nauwtice of yaw nauwts!" Easy to remember. Thank you, Dr. Lush!

As you have led the way to Glory, someday I'll thank you in person.

Take care of the minutes, and the hours will take care of themselves. G.K. Chesterton

Ordered Up from the Farm

Army Staff Sergeant George Whitley looked and acted like a squared-away soldier when I, as civilian command information officer, worked with him at the Office of Chief, Public Affairs, at Headquarters U.S. Army Europe in Heidelberg. George, who couldn't disguise his southern accent, was a farm boy who hailed from Andy Griffith country, a farm a few hours' drive from Raleigh, N.C.

George told me of his life on a farm, sometimes taking a hunting dog and spending several days in an abandoned cabin acres away from the farmhouse, shooting his food and contemplating life under the hot Carolina sun. No such thing as indoor dogs or cats on the farm, he said.

One day, similar to the classic black-and-white Andy Griffith movie, George got his notice to report for an induction physical. Coupons covering the cost of the bus ride and one night in a hotel accompanied the letter.

With a sense of duty to his country, George boarded the bus, rode several hours to Raleigh and checked into the hotel.

The next morning, after a good night's sleep, he arose early and began dressing to report to the induction center.

It was nearly 24 hours since he departed the farmhouse to start his overnight journey.

Buttoning his shirt, he looked down to his bare feet.

Without too much concern he entertained a fleeting thought.

"I wonder if I should have brought shoes."

The Communist Price Was Right

An intriguing trip to take in Germany was to board the Army's free duty train, climb into a bunk and ride by night through Communist East Germany to Berlin. Peek through the curtain and see the ominous-looking Soviet soldiers beside the track.

One trip, I checked into my compartment only to find a female soldier there. Nothing surprised her; she figured she'd take the top bunk in this man's Army. I found the arrangement troubling, and the conductor spotted the mistake and reassigned her to another compartment.

Several times, however, I was able to take Suzanne and Mike on the trip. Good buddy J.B. Kump and family were stationed in Berlin, and we enjoyed visiting them. We ventured into East Berlin, where ice cream cones and Cokes were a nickel each—just like boyhood days. East Berlin had its own Space Needle—a restaurant atop a tower. I treated the Kumps and my family to a steak dinner up there, with all the fixings. For seven people, the meals were a dollar a person. We enjoyed the inexpensive experience so much that we decided to order dessert.

"I'm sorry," the disciplined Communist waiter said with a frown.

"Your time limit is up."

A Painful Lesson Their Gums
Will Never Forget

My first computer was a Commodore 64 which, as I recall, I bought at the Canadian Post Exchange in Germany in the early 1980s. I also bought their dot matrix printer, and I used these to type up my notes for sermons I gave at the Heidelberg Friday Night Fellowship.

One day, Suzanne looked over the notes coming out of the printer. They were a bit hard to read, because the "descenders," the tails on the "g," "j," "p," "q" and "y" printed out above the line instead of dipping below, as we are used to seeing them.

I had written about the suffering the Apostle Paul and his companion endured as recorded in Acts 16: *The crowd joined in the attack against Paul and Silas, and the magistrates ordered them to be stripped and beaten. After they had been severely flogged, they were thrown into prison.*

That primitive printer made it look like something else, with those tails jammed higher on the line. To Suzanne, the "g" looked like "s."

She tried to read it aloud: "After they had been severely *flossed...*"

We are so fortunate to have the Gospel, the Good News that St. Paul carried far and wide. If it were I, I think I may have given up, especially after being flossed within an inch of my life! How does one recover from such cruel and unusual punishment?

Paul often talked about a "thorn in the flesh"—a health problem he would not divulge. From this reading, it could very well have been bleeding gums.

Baseball Giant Taught Me the World's Best Investment

Lt. Col. Stan Witter served with me as a public affairs officer in the Washington Air National Guard. Call him selfless. He recommended my selection to share his position, even though it meant he'd have to retire shortly by sharing the job with a younger man. Just that act alone said a great deal about this special guy.

I learned Stan's two sons were serving as press secretaries for two congressmen. They had followed their dad in his chosen profession of journalism. Stan had been a news anchor for a Spokane television station.

His sons and daughter were staunch admirers of their father. What kind of a man deserves such devotion and adoration that even his sons want to grow up to be just like him?

I learned one reason. When his sons were small, Stan signed them up for Little League baseball. His boys were on the same team. The older boy got to play all the time, but the younger boy spent most of his time on the bench.

We've heard about unruly and obnoxious Little League parents. Not Stan, even though the bench time broke his heart. He decided to remedy this situation without badgering the coach.

He withdrew all his savings—$500. "I bought a Little League team," he said. Well, he became sponsor. The short-term result was that both boys played in every game. But his life savings was a small price to pay for the lifetime bene-fits—the admiring eyes of sons who saw their dad as a man who would sacrifice all for his boys, the man who forever will remain a giant, their greatest hero.

It was the best investment he ever made.

Fun-loving Commanders?

Most commanders I've worked for knew how to have fun. The ones who succeeded mastered the art of balancing lighthearted fun with business. My sensors may have needed a little adjustment through the years. I was either a bit hesitant to let my hair down among the brass, or I overdid it a bit.

One colonel asked the transportation squadron commander to see about painting all the vehicles on base in preparation for the upcoming high headquarters vehicle inspection. The Barney-Fife-type captain read the regulations and reported back.

"The regulation says we can only touch up the vehicles, Sir," the captain said.

"OK, then touch them up all over," the colonel ordered.

Colonel Keplinger at Fairchild Air Force Base, Spokane, Wash., loved to play practical jokes on the generals. For the general's family housing inspection, "Kep" ordered one of the vacant quarters parched lawns to be painted green and hoped the general's route would include Kep's "artwork" in the inspection.

Air Force bases don't generally have Howitzer cannons, but Kep wanted one. He had airmen set off a charge every day at retreat.

One day Kep ordered a parade of all the airmen on base and invited the general to stand on a trailer bed as the airmen passed in review. At just the right time, Kep had arranged for airmen to sneak the Howitzer in behind the trailer. When it was time for the National Anthem, the Howitzer belched out an earthshaking B-O-O-O-M!!! Dust a pebbles few! The poor general's heart had to skip a beat or two, but he had to remain composed at the position of attention!

A deputy commander in the Corps wanted to be honored at the Fort Lewis retirement parade on his last day. But he made too many trips around our building foraging for cookies and candy. An officer was banned from a retirement parade if he was on the "fat boy" program. So we threw a banquet in his honor, got up from our tables and marched around the banquet hall just for him.

Colonel Tim Wynn enjoyed a lighthearted moment. Like Jack Benny, I often tried to entertain employees at a "Town Hall" with sour notes on my trombone. Once I filled my trombone with water and emptied it so that some drizzled on the colonel's shoe. He got back at me, and as a result I got my most prized

93

appraisal. It's part of my permanent record. No evaluation from a colonel was ever so eloquent:

"Plays a lousy trombone."

Some commanders had a warped sense of humor. I'll withhold the names to protect the innocent. One colonel's idea of "fun" was to exploit one's fears. A civilian manager's fear manifested itself at high elevations and in helicopters. Learning of this fear, the colonel ordered the manager to go with him on a helicopter ride. He had arranged for Vietnam-trained pilots to avoid a gradual descent and instead, they turned off the engine high overhead and auto-rotated to the ground. The manager panicked and screamed all the way down. Just before the chopper hit the ground, the pilot started the engine and landed the craft. The manager had wet his pants.

The colonel laughed uproariously, and the manager had to be restrained from assaulting his commanding officer with a barrage of curses and fisticuffs.

Most of those "old-school" madmen, thank goodness, have since been drummed out of the service.

Phony Dividing Wall

Don't get me wrong. I really don't think I treat employees with bias. In fact, backed up with awards for hiring equitably, I've been told I offered the most equal employment opportunity in the Corps' Seattle District.

But one exercise during Cultural Awareness Week rubbed me the wrong way. An outside speaker conducted the activity. She asked a couple dozen members of the audience to form a circle.

"If you went to a private grade school," she said, "take one step forward."

"If any of your family ever spent time in a detention camp, take one step backward."

"If you went to a private high school, take one step forward."

"If you are a person of color, take one step backward."

"If you went to a private college, take one step forward."

"If you have an advanced degree, take one step forward."

As I recall, she had us step backward if we had parents or grandparents who never received more than a third-grade education, and other socioeconomic distinctions.

Two women, as well as Phil O'Dell, Chief of Engineering, and me—who are white males—were left in the middle, in what she later described as "the inner circle of success."

Just before she tried to drive the lesson home, as if to manipulate the results, she said, "If you are a woman, take two steps back."

Her intention was to show that economic success was available, without exception, to white males only.

Baloney. I certainly understand the point. Women, minorities and people from poorer backgrounds have more of a struggle. I was one of those. But to portray a scenario in which it was impossible for one of these to succeed—I thought the notion to be disingenuous.

We all overcome obstacles in life. Some face more barriers to others. But the moment one suggests success is utterly *impossible*, I call a personal foul.

Fifteen yards for unsportsmanlike conduct.

The Lure of Twinkies

I never cared much for Twinkies. I've eaten maybe 10 in my life. But they have irresistible power over some people.

Take son Michael, for example. I took him to work when I taught journalism at Fort Harrison. The cafeteria had just installed a bunch of vending machines and a microwave. Microwaves were something of a novelty then, and I wanted to find something for Mike to eat that he'd enjoy heating up. He's a bit of a picky eater, so the only thing I found was a package of Twinkies.

I was horrified. After a few seconds of nuking, the white crème (lard and sugar) turned into a clear liquid. Another dumb idea.

After we choked those things down, I took Mike to class and began teaching. He looked bored. Finally we drove home, and he said very little. I was sorry I had shown him such a dreary day at the "office."

Two weeks later he asked, "Hey, Dad, when can we go to your work again and heat up some more Twinkies!"

Go figure.

Then there was Ford Hubbert, a short-statured giant of a children's pastor at Aurora Church of the Nazarene. I called him the Pied Piper, because he could go nowhere in the church without eight or 10 kids following him. They loved that man. He would take them on long bike rides and encourage them to bring Twinkies for energy. Sometimes he'd take the children down to Union Gospel Mission to brighten the days of the homeless people.

Everyone was deeply saddened the day Ford announced his resignation. His pastor-buddy had accepted a call to a church in Colorado and he wanted Ford to minister to the children there.

Ford's Aurora kids wanted to throw a farewell party. They had him sit on a throne and put a crown on his head. Dozens of children had written heart-rending tributes, and they recited them for him. Many of them included a gift of Twinkies, Ford's trademark. Soon the throne was piled high with the silly snacks.

Tears welled up in Ford's eyes, and in ours, too.

The next week I was invited to help with Communion. Ford was sitting next to me. Jokingly, I said, "Welcome back."

But it was true. Pastor Tharon Daniels announced that Ford withdrew his resignation. He stayed with his extended family of adoring children in Seattle. Wild cheering and applause.

It was the mountain of Twinkies, of course, that won back his big heart.

Saint Chuck

Despite the many triumphs of service achieved by my in-laws, the Johnson family, they knew many dark days of struggle and tragedy. After serving as missionaries in South Africa, Warren continued to serve the Lord as a Free Methodist pastor. Skilled in working toward reconciliation among troubled churches, the denomination gave him a number of short-term assignments to churches facing difficult situations. In a number of those situations, Warren used his gift to bring a peaceful and loving solution—a gift passed on to his son in bringing about brotherhood arising from the ashes of dispute.

How could this be—trouble in the Body of Christ, the church? It's an old misconception that Satan loves to feed, that people in churches are somehow superhuman and not subject to the temptations and weaknesses of "ordinary" people. Unchurched people point to imperfections among Christians and holler, "Hypocrites!" Sure, you can find the counterfeit among the genuine article in any institution, and certainly the church is no exception, as the scriptures portray. Truth is, the real mission of a church is not to serve as a shrine for perfect saints, but as a hospital for broken people. It is only when we become aware of our shortcomings and learn humility that Christ can provide the necessary healing. Or we may be doing nothing wrong, and God is "pruning" us for a greater mission.

Even so, becoming a pastor or missionary certainly doesn't exempt us from enemy attack. No doubt the forces of evil work triple time to try to derail one who has most committed himself or herself to God's service. Here I hasten to say that God's service encompasses far more than pastors or missionaries; the God of the universe has commissioned light-and-comfort-bearing janitors, seamstresses, clerks, athletes, homemakers, pipe-fitters, teachers, stockbrokers, medical workers, analysts, soldiers, waiters, actors and, yes, even those who are attorneys and public affairs officers—none without crisis, heartache and struggle amidst the glory.

Among Rev. Warren and Jean Johnson's four unique and gifted children, Janet garnered perhaps the most attention. This dark-haired, square-jawed beauty had piercing, inquisitive eyes and a radiant smile. This special daughter attracted an uncommon man, Chuck, one whose devotion to her rivaled that of perhaps any spouse in history and played out in magnitude of Biblical proportions.

Janet, who would in due course live out more than one earthly life, was diagnosed as a schizophrenic. Learning what to call her sometimes strange behavior, the family rallied to provide the support she needed. The towering love she got from her godly parents was, perhaps, to be expected. But the love story lived out by husband Chuck was legendary.

I met Chuck even before I met Janet. He was a fun-loving man, full of life and energy, with a heart for God. Good thing. He was to need divine resources in massive doses. Janet was a delightful, giving Christian woman when she was on her medicine for the proper length of time. But off the medicine, she'd assume the identity of a stranger in a black leather jacket. She took on another name, complete with ID card and even a man she regarded as her significant other, who lived in Tacoma Chuck was amazingly patient and loving throughout the many flair-ups of the illness, but when Janet's missionary family discovered her assumed name and alliance, they came to Chuck and said they could fully understand how he could be at the end of his rope. Though there was talk of hanging in there, at least some of the family came to the realization that Chuck had their understanding if he were to sever the relationship and move on.

But this Saint was not ready to surrender. Convinced that he had a lifelong commitment to a "covenant marriage," he frequented Tacoma and looked up Janet's other personality's male interest. Patiently, firmly and only by the grace of God, Chuck was able to let his inner light shine to such an extent that it melted the heart of the "other" man. He and Chuck began studying scriptures together and, incredibly, actually became friends. A lost but perhaps seeking soul, confronted by a genuine Christlike life displayed simply and openly just may be more than ready to give up sin's entrapments and addictions, swapping them for the joy that comes from a timeless message and practice. Others, astonished at Chuck's prophet-like perseverance, were stunned at the news that Chuck had simply led the man to become a transformed child of God. Before it even sank in with the family, the man came across a scriptural passage, privately turned to Janet and said, "I read in God's Word that you have little choice but to go back to your husband."

Janet did, was restored, and though she had occasional relapses and other identities, she forever put the memory of the man behind her. She and Chuck enjoyed a number of good times in their marriage. After a few years, Janet began to believe that she was being healed. She slowly and secretly, without concurrence from a physician, weaned herself off the medicine…and for several days, suddenly disappeared.

I wasn't aware of the disappearance. The Johnson family attempted to deal with this latest ordeal quietly with the authorities. One day I heard on the news that a woman had walked herself in front of a bus and died. It was sad, I thought, yet another of a daily broadcast menu of personal tragedies. Nor did the "routine" news trigger alarm among most of Janet's family—except John. A red flag went up in his mind's eye. He called the coroner on Sunday morning and arranged to meet him at the morgue. The coroner didn't know who this woman was. John thought there was a chance he might recognize the body.

He worst fear was correct. The body was Janet's.

Saint Chuck has shed many tears since that day and suffered still more sadness, but he is a rock of faithfulness to his God. When my way is rough, I feel singularly blessed that someone like Chuck crossed my path to so vividly demonstrate that Christ is not an icon or myth, but Reality within—only when He is invited—Who is a steady, living source of strength and endurance, such that passes all understanding. I pray for Chuck that God will reward him richly in this life and the in the next for being an ordinary man who tapped extraordinary power in order to be an overcomer when a lesser person or lesser faith like mine might easily have given up.

Truly, Chuck, to me you are, as another saint, Peter, said, one of *His own special people, that you may proclaim the praises of Him who called you out of darkness into His marvelous light.*

Holiest Place

What's the holiest place or moment you've ever known or heard about?

When I was a kid I thought it was when our 6-foot-6 bachelor Pastor Wally Roseberg prayed on his knees from 5 to 7 o'clock every morning. Or hearing of my prayer-warrior grandmother praying on her knees in front of an overstuffed chair for her nine children and dozens of grandchildren...or seeing my dad and mom doing the same thing. Such sights and stories filled me with awe.

Before I was confirmed and invited to take part in communion, I thought the Lord's Table just might be the most sacred event.

So many things at King's Garden, the miracle place where I went to high school, filled me with reverence: the story of founder Mike Martin claiming the 40-acre property in his bare feet—*Every place whereon the soles of your feet shall tread shall be yours.* Deuteronomy 11:24. Then, when many well-heeled individuals and organizations were anxious to bid on the place, Mike put his finger on the passage claiming the promise to *close the mouths of the lions* and won the bid for the property with just $1 over minimum. Or could the holiest time be the sacred sound of perhaps 100 King's Garden workers praying aloud simultaneously kneeling in front of their chapel seats.

Or how about the hushed and trembling times listening to camp testimonies before a campfire?

The holiest place and time I ever heard about was the day Dad died in July 1994. The time and place was the folks' tiny apartment in Poulsbo, where Mom spent her first night alone, while her soul mate had entered heaven's gates. I heard the next day that Mom was unable to sleep that entire night. Still an accomplished singer, she filled the lonely night hours by singing hymn after hymn and reading scriptures. I listen to her lead the family in carols or hymns at holiday celebrations, and these are special times, but not as awe-inspiring as that night after Dad died. Was Mom's only audience God Himself? It was her Command Performance. I like to think Dad was listening, too, from heaven's balcony.

Yes, I am convinced—that bedroom was the holiest, most sacred time and place I know.

No Lights, No Running Water
Until She Smelled a Rat

I called Jan Spicer, my commuting buddy, "Pioneer Woman." She met her husband on Mt. McKinley, Alaska, where the couple lived without electricity or running water. Trim the wicks and carry the water.

The couple moved to a wooded area of Poulsbo, Washington, where they carried on the pioneer life routine until Jan became pregnant. At long last they installed electrical circuits and a pump where they had dug a well.

Baby came along just fine, thank you, illuminated, healthy and happy. After a few months, Mom was giving Baby a sip of orange juice. Jan sniffed it—it smelled bad. She went to the faucet and smelled a glass of water. It reeked.

She told Hubby, who immediately climbed down with a flashlight to take a closer look at the well.

What's that at the bottom—a cat?

It was a black, dead rat, as big as a cat.

The family moved in with friends while Hubby spent a week scrubbing down the well from top to bottom with Clorox.

Think you have problems? At least when you have a nightmare, you can wake up and you're relieved to know it didn't actually happen that way.

It was not a mere nightmare for Jan and her family. They had to deal with it. But the adversity made them, from then on, a little stronger—and a whole lot more alert.

Just Tell Me Where
You Want to Go

During the first Gulf War, I received two medals.

Before the shooting started, while serving in Operation Desert Storm, my assignment was to escort a Spokane TV crew to Jeddah, Saudi Arabia, and put them up for a week in the Hyatt Regency Hotel.

When we drove to a nearby Saudi base to videotape members of the Air Guard, I forgot one of the three passes I needed to clear security. A U.S. Air Guard technical sergeant decided he'd try to "talk" our way through the checkpoints, heavily guarded by the Saudi military.

"He's with me," he'd tell the guards.

One guard wasn't buying it. He said nothing but first pointed at me and gestured for me to follow him. He called for a Saudi vehicle and I was driven to another compound. No American in sight. I was detained in silent solitude for perhaps less than an hour, but it seemed like an eternity. Finally, an American Air Guard security officer appeared and sprung me from "captivity."

Back at the hotel, we had tried several of their international restaurants—Chinese food in Saudi Arabia! We asked about dining in one of the local restaurants. The desk clerk advised us to stick with one of the hotels. He said a number of Americans frequented the Marriott Hotel in Jeddah.

About eight of us piled into two cabs. I told the cabbie, "Marriott Hotel, please."

He nodded and drove around for 10 minutes.

"Mah-rriott?" He didn't speak a word of English.

I nodded. "Yes, Marriott Hotel, please."

He drove another five minutes.

"Mah-rriott?"

"Yes! Marriott Hotel!"

He drove to where a group of cabbies were standing around smoking. Our cabbie asked them where the hotel was. No one seemed to know. He drove us another five minutes.

"Mah-rriott?"

"Yes, please! Marriott Hotel!"

He found a sheik dressed in flowing white robes and talked to him.

The sheik approached our cab and spoke in perfect English.

"Where is it you would like to go?"

"The Marriott Hotel, please." The sheik spoke briefly to our cabbie, whose face lit up.

"Ah! Mah-rri-OAT!"

We happily arrived in two minutes.

The Freedom of Letting Go

Would you ask for more adversity? No, I suppose not. And yet, little or no spiritual progress results except through suffering. We don't want to hear that. We don't thank God for the affliction, but we can always praise Him in the midst of it. No matter how painful or difficult, we can always think of someone who has had a more difficult time. And we can find blessings to count. Can we learn to relax, to enter God's rest, no matter what? I remember Larry King asking Billy Graham one of my greatest fears, whether he worries that he might die in a plane crash. "I'm ready to do that, if God so chooses." What a simple truth. Adopting it as my own, it helped me relax about many of my concerns about what the future may hold.

Some time ago I read of a man who experienced flutters in his chest and each time feared the sensation signaled his imminent death. Telling a counselor, the advice he got startled him: "Next time you feel the flutters, just say, 'Bring them on.' Let the flutters do whatever they want—yes, even take your life, if need be. Ready or not, it's now or never."

He followed the advice, and neither his fear nor the flutters ever reappeared.

For our light and momentary troubles are achieving for us an eternal glory that far outweighs them all. 2 Corinthians 4:17 (NIV)

Washington, Churchill and Me: Enjoying a Charmed Life

As a boy, I had heard the story of Winston Churchill, described as living a charmed life, having escaped many a life-threatening tragedy. Later I learned that George Washington experienced similar providential protection, even when Indians had zeroed in on him as an easy target during the French and Indian War. The Chief later was determined to visit this man, whose life the Great Spirit had spared repeatedly. The great Hebrew warrior, King David, was also spared by God.

Oh, but my thoughts turn to D-Day. Listen to those older vets talk about their experiences at Normandy. Tears. Quavering voices that choke off words after well more than a half century. One vet said he had been trained to seek out trees or rocks as cover. On Omaha beach he found none, and so for cover he pulled dead bodies over himself. He returned a half-century later to face his haunting feeling of cowardice.

I saw the former airborne soldiers, some in their 80s, return to risk life and limb and reenact their jump once again.

And I thought of my own military career, 12 years of active duty and 16 years as a reservist, seeing duty in California, Japan, Korea, Spokane, Indianapolis, Italy, Germany, Tacoma and Saudi Arabia.

As Carl Sandburg recalls,

> *Ten thousand men and boys twist on their bodies in a red soak along a river edge,*
> *Gasping of wounds, calling for water, some rattling death in their throats.*
> *Who would guess what it cost...*

What they did enabled my duty to resemble a tourist's vacation. During Desert Shield, the Air Force gave me two ribbons for escorting media from Spokane, stopping in Spain, to Jeddah, Saudi Arabia, where we lodged in luxury at the Hyatt Regency.

I have viewed myself something of a hawk for most of my life. But, as I reflect on D-Day, it is often others whom I envision on the attack. Wading ashore in water up to my neck only to see my buddies struck all around me from machine gunfire is a thought that horrifies me. It is true: Far from war-mongering, no one wants peace more than the person who puts his or her life on the line. I didn't even come close. I never had to test my own cowardice. And to me, that tearful vet who in fear pulled dead bodies over himself is far more a hero than I'll ever be. Because of him, I am unscarred, unscathed.

Move over, Winston, King David and George—I share names with two of you, but I cannot begin to compare your feats of battle. Yet I, David George Harris, honored as you by God with a "charmed life," am of all veterans most richly blest.

Air Traffic Control Stranger

Who'd have thought you could see this dazzling aerial performance on the decks of the Bainbridge ferry?

The air traffic controller looks like an orchestra conductor, despite his tattered jacket. He deftly pulls a Cheez-it from his pocket and sleek birds assume their formation. They hover, methodically maneuvering for their assigned spot. If one of the seagulls hesitates before reaching his rendezvous, the controller waves him off. Another gull fills the slot and takes the prize from the outstretched hand. Six to 10 birds participate every day.

The controller speaks, waves, coaxes the birds into position. He will not tolerate the slightest imprecision. Each bird knows his place in the upper-deck que.

"Regulars" watch in awe but dare not attempt the concerto themselves. They leave the performance to the master and his fledglings.

During the summer tourist season, it's another story. Little and big boys and girls beg their mommies for the bait.

They never get it right. The tourists attempt to conduct the flock with pitiful substitutes like popcorn or potato chips. The flyers show their contempt. Even if the tourists choose the right incentive food, their arm motions betray the amateurs. The birds reveal their confusion and ineptness.

What the master achieved, the efforts of the tourists result only in birds crashing into one another or and collapsing the breathless symmetry of the well-crafted formation.

The tourists end their strivings in aviation failure, the controller returns from intermission and resumes the air show. Instantly the gulls recognize the master and form up to resume their dinner-show artistry.

You end your voyage humbled at the opportunity of witnessing the historical wonder of the age. These are the creatures of speechless grace who, without so much as a word, taught the Wright Brothers the secrets of flight.

Precision Talent

One night in a cold, wet, dark Navy parking lot I witnessed spectacular precision talent.

I work in media relations. It sounds glamorous, but it's more scary than glitzy. At any moment terrible events totally out of my control can thrust me into the limelight. I dread the day I'm expected to answer, "live," questions about a disaster I know little about.

Media relations require little in the way of talent. Maybe that's why I chose this field. I don't mean to put down my hard-working peers. But that's how to succeed in my business: plain, hard work. Connecting the dots. Documenting a lot of ordinary or technical conversations. I translate what engineers and scientists say into plain English. That's not talent, at least not in my case. It's being simple-minded. If I can understand what the scientist says, anyone can. If I can't understand it, she needs to say it in another way.

What I saw in the rainy parking lot simply awed me. The feeling was not unlike the greasy master craftsman who merely sniffed the dipstick and told me everything wrong with my '73 Olds Cutlass automatic transmission. Simply awesome.

Last night the talent was every bit as stunning. At the Navy grocery store, the commissary, baggers don't get paid unless you tip them. One high school bagger was having the time of his life. He had two carts piled high with groceries. He grabbed the carts, back-to-back, and started running. He then jumped aboard between the carts and rode them across the street. Then he did it again. And again.

I thought of how it would be if I did it, even at his age. One of the carts would crash into a Beemer. I'd fall off the other and it would run over my toe and then my neck. All my life inanimate objects have conspired against me. It happens in the morning when I'm using my hair dryer. If I wanted to, I could never swing the cord and hook it on anything. But when I don't want it to happen, the cord hooks the drawer and pulls it out, while knocking the deodorant, toothpaste, shaver and brush to the floor.

Talent. That high school kid had amazing eye-to-hand motor skills. He had to align the eight wheels of those carts with breathtaking exactitude, and he did so effortlessly, without a thought. That baggy-pants, rebellious twerp was beautiful, simply beautiful to watch.

Nobody ever said that about my stammering on-camera sound bites.

Gangland Pillaging of Our Happy Home

What an awesome burden of senseless irresponsibility. I will have been held accountable for the night's systematic gangland intrusion and devastation of our picturesque home overlooking peaceful Hood Canal and the majestic Olympic Mountains.

It had begun only a few hours before. The ringing telephone broke through the laughter of my granddaughters' play as they visited their grandparents. The voice on the other end was clipped.

"Don't ask any questions. Meet my bus at the park-and-ride in Poulsbo. I'm at the Bainbridge Island ferry terminal, and I have no keys."

My wife, Suzanne, quickly arranged for the care of the grandchildren with their visiting great grandmother and sped to her husband's rescue.

"What happened?"

"I went to the Corps picnic, ended up in the dunk-the-boss tank, changed my trousers and hung the wet ones on a tree to dry. That's where they remain, with my keys."

"What if someone finds tem?"

"How will they know whose they are?"

"Is there no other identification?"

"No. I have my wallet with me."

"Think, Dave. Someone may know it was your organization and know you were the one in the dunk-the-boss tank."

"Not to worry, then, because at least 20 bosses took their turn to be dunked."

Thinking I had put the issue to rest, I flipped on the TV at home, not anticipating my wife's final, horrifying and cold, indicting question that unlocked the mystery and pointed the gangster spotlight right in my face. Immediately, I began making plans to evacuate my family moments before the arrival of the marauding thieves and murderers....

"But how many of those 20," she asked gravely, "hung their pants in the tree?"

Freak Line Asks, "Who's Your President?"

Somehow Public Affairs got stuck with the "Freak Line" for the Corps of Engineers' Seattle District. That's what we call the switchboard. Someone thought we knew most of the answers to callers' questions, so we got the freak line added to our already busy duties fielding media calls and the like.

The mostly civilian Corps of Engineers is listed under "U.S. Army," so we get such questions as, "How can I get my child support from my soldier husband?" Or, "I need to talk to someone about a serious threat to our country, due to a conspiracy involving the CIA."

Ooh boy.

My favorite caller was a young man with a deep voice trying to sell something or gather executive names for some promotion.

"Would you say your company's annual sales are more that $1 million, $5 million or $10 million?"

"This is not a company. It is the federal government."

"Who is your CEO?"

"Colonel Ralph Graves."

"Who is the Chief Financial Officer of your company?"

"This is not a company. It is the federal government."

"What is the name of your president?"

"George W. Bush."

"Is he local?"

"No. He lives in the White House in Washington, D.C."

"Who is your principal owner?"

"You, the taxpayer, are one of the owners."

"When is your annual stockholder meet…"

<Click>

I Needed To Send That $50 Money Order

For years it kept nagging me. A clear conscience eluded me.

Bill Gothard is a devout man who would go all over the country and, in a plainspoken, quiet way present a practical plan for intimacy...with God. Bill's unpretentious presentations drew tens of thousands of people in big city arenas.

I didn't always agree with everything he said, but I'd be better off if I followed more of his example. I was inspired by his commitment. He demonstrated what a difference one could make in people's lives through closeness with God and a willingness to put legs on one's faith. Bill worked with street kids earlier in his career. Co-workers asked him why he dressed so nice on the streets and didn't "dress down" like the street kids.

"I want to show them something better that they can attain," he said, "not a mirror image of the destructive life they have been living."

In his seminars I learned that I could not make much progress unless I had a clear conscience. Bill challenged us to think back in our past and to make amends with anyone we had offended. He discouraged the use of letters. If possible, we were to make an appointment with the person and ask, "Can you find it in your heart to forgive me?"

Sometimes a personal visit to someone I offended is impractical, but it's a good idea.

God had reminded me of an unresolved debt during my college years. A friend of my dad's in church, Bill Boyd, had had a 1953 Pontiac just like mine, and he had a couple tires hanging in his garage. My tires were bald, and my dad asked if he'd part with the tires for a reasonable price. Bill said, "Sure," and I came and got them. Dad said I should give him $10.

Twenty-five years later, I still had not gotten around to forking over the money, and I lived thousands of miles away. But every time I thought about a clear conscience, God reminded me that I still owed Bill. By then, that $10 was probably worth $50.

I had heard someone else try something that moved me to action. I sent a check from Indianapolis to Mom in Seattle, where Bill lived. I asked Mom to cash the check, buy a postal money order for $50, and send it to Bill.

I told her to sign it, "I M BROTHER."

Since then I wondered what happened. I'm sure Mom sent it to Bill. Perhaps Bill opened it and thought it was some kind of ad or promotion. Maybe he ripped it up and threw it away. "What a waste," I thought.

No. It didn't matter what Bill did with that money order. It was I who needed to do what I needed to do.

And this time, I obeyed God and did it.

Mighty and Good Two-Coupon Ticket

I attended a larger Baptist church near home in Indianapolis. Excited at the academic prowess and innovative note display of the pastor, it sounded like mighty good preaching. I was half right. It was good. Not mighty. I can't remember one thing that was said. After the services, the pastor disappeared. I had to make an appointment just to shake his hand.

After I met Suzanne we attended a church where the preaching lacked zip but displayed more emotion. In fact, if people praised and shouted enough, folks thought it just fine if the emotion squeezed out the preaching altogether. "Wow! We had church!" That's what they'd want us to think if the preaching could be set aside for another week. The preacher used to say, "I feel good all over more than anywhere else." Friends would get together after Sunday night service, eat butterscotch squares, and mimic that phrase. Later we discovered the preacher fell from grace, and we left that church for Northview Christian Center, the greatest church I've ever known—or maybe it was Pastor Tommy. We'd chuckle about the other pastor who still remained with the old church. "Now we know why he felt better all over more than anywhere else!"

Northview, led by Tommy Paino, had just the right balance. Tommy was a lover of people, and his congregation grew from 32 to 1,400 in a matter of months. Here was the real thing.

My buddy Gene knew the difference. Gene had no academic credentials, but he was wise beyond his years, listening intently and absorbing powerful nuggets of truth from truly great expositors.

"Jesus explains it the fourth chapter of John," Gene said. "He told us that 'God is Spirit, and those who worship must worship in spirit and in truth.' That Baptist church—not the same with all Baptists—had the truth, but not much spirit. The other old church had a lot of spirit, but less emphasis on truth. Tommy powerfully preaches the truth, and at the same time he leads us in appropriate spirited worship." My buddy had thus described Tommy's sensitivity to faithfully maintaining a fine-tuned balance. Gene drove the point home by quoting Paul's first letter to the Corinthians. *But everything should be done in a fitting and orderly way... The spirits of prophets are subject to the control of prophets.*

Gene's sound teaching of John and First Corinthians stuck with me like few sermons have. Tommy emphasized not "tongues," or "wonders" or "signs." But he exhibited and preached the "baptism of power" and of genuine *agape* love, unconditional, not expecting anything in return.

I love the memory of the late, great Tommy, with whom I ran the Indy 500 Mini-Marathon. A few years later, God needed him to add his spirit and love in heaven. Tommy died of Lou Gehrig's disease.

But it was my friend Gene, who in the comfort of home preached the most powerful sermon about worshiping in both spirit and in truth.

Thanks to Gene, I know the difference between "mighty" and "good."

Hoosier Humble

The way my Indiana friends carried on about my advanced degree, you'd think that was key to our relationship. Oh, I hope not. I was a blest man for the privilege of having the Air Force provide a free ride on that one.

I think the ingredients that made this special circle of friends click were these: they first came to love my caring wife—they knew her as "Sue"—and they naturally wanted to include me for her sake. But then, mutual discovery sustained those relationships. As Sue describes me, "You may be intelligent, but you have no common sense." In other words, she and the others found me to be not a stuffy academic, but a down-to-earth, fun-loving guy, somewhat awkward and with plenty of foibles. On their part, I found them, like Sue, to not only enjoy fun, but also they had wisdom, knowledge and understanding that, frankly, kept me in awe. I would sometimes lead little homilies or try to make an audible prayer somewhat articulate, and they'd good naturedly tease me about it afterwards. That kept me humble. One time the pastor asked me to lead in prayer, and I felt overwhelmed by the abundance of God's Word in America—so many English translations—opportunity everywhere one looked to hear from God and to read what He had to say. In awkward terms, I tried to thank Him for all those opportunities and versions.

My Indy buddies were merciless! Again eating munchies that Sunday night, Gene tried to mimic my prayer, with plenty of license to embellish: "Lord, we're so thankful tonight for the New International Version," he began. "And tonight we especially want to mention the Revised Standard Version, along with the Living Bible. And lest we forget those versions who could not be with us this evening—the Amplified Bible and the New American Standard Version. May we be true to the King James Version. In Thy Name we pray. Amen." Uproarious laughter.

Irreverent? Not if you knew these God-fearing Hoosiers. It was their loving way of telling me to get off my high horse—or how refreshing it was that their "educated" friend often spoke in common or silly ways and stumbled over his words like everyone else.

The mutual respect gelled as I was often reminded and humbled by their keen insight—no chance for uppity behavior on my part—confirmed by the words of Dr. Luke in the Book of Acts: *When they saw the courage of Peter and John and realized that they were unschooled, ordinary men, they were astonished and they took note that these men had been with Jesus.* Or perhaps, again, by Paul in I Corinthians: *For the foolishness of God is wiser than man's wisdom, and the weakness of God is stronger than man's strength.... The man without the Spirit does not accept the things that come from the Spirit of God, for they are foolishness to him, and he cannot understand them, because they are spiritually discerned.*

What are you Going to Hell for?

I heard a TV pastor speak on all the reasons people use to reject God and go to hell. He had a number of props suggesting a variety of means to moral failure. Some would choose promiscuous sex or substance abuse instead of heaven. "I'm going to hell so I can cheat Uncle Sam out of $300."

I have often thought of that sermon, and I think of those around me who may choose to go to hell for other reasons as well. I asked Roger and Michele on the ferry why they rejected Christianity. Michele offered the reason that an uncle prohibited playing cards in his home. Which was silliest? Banning the cards, or using that as an excuse to screw up her eternal destiny?

Imagine. "I'd rather go to hell than put up with Uncle Bill's narrow-minded view of playing cards." Flawless thinking? Is there a way to engage Bill in a loving dialogue or find a better instrument of interaction than the disputed cards?

The ones I'm most concerned about, however, are friends I know who are good people. They live lives of integrity. They give of their time and money to charity. They fight for the downtrodden and wouldn't think of living anything but an upstanding life.

Those are the toughest to reach for God. They believe they will make it to heaven based on their performance. And yet God has said that all have sinned and have come short of the glory of God, that committing one wrong makes us guilty of all.

Will such a good person live a whole life of virtue and end up in eternal, conscious, agonizing separation from God—a fate of their own making?

God says yes. Why??? Because He will have no other gods before Him. And choosing "goodness" apart from integrating our whole lives in Him to be transformed is choosing our own agenda, and that is idolatry—self-deification, self-worship. We all must choose to worship, and there are only two options: we worship the One God, or we worship what? Everything else—secular humanism, eastern religions, "New Age"—they all comprise the second choice, self-worship. Yes, even if our entire life is spent duplicating the compassionate work of Mother Teresa, it falls short of a holy God and declares we can create or selectively observe our own rules and pursue the goal on our own. We want to leave God out of the picture.

Dallas Willard says it is simply a matter of God giving you your preferences when you pass form this life. If you've avoided God all your life, if you've chosen to separate yourself from Him, He won't force you to live with Him. Hell could be nothing more or less than a desolate planet somewhere in the universe. I don't want that kind of loneliness.

Oh, reader, if this is you wanting to be your own god, think of the awful price—self-imposed tortuous regret for an eternity. Our only hope is redemption, calling upon Jesus to indwell us, to save us, to transform us, to give us a new outlook—the mind of Christ. He alone paid the price. God is love and joy, and without Him in every compartment of our lives, we're sunk. Submitting our lives to Him brings eternal joy, starting today. *At Thy right hand there are joys forevermore.* I need not wait for death to taste glory. I have it today.

Dear Reader, if you've known me to exude joy and bliss, it is when I let God be God within and allow Him on the throne of my heart to direct my every action. Those times when you see me angry or cynical, it is when I have nudged Him off my heart's throne and grabbed the steering wheel. It's no fun when I do that.

Thank God He forgives me. I give Him back the wheel and I can resume the joyride. What are you waiting for? What are you going to hell for? Some elusive pleasure? There's the irony. The greatest pleasures I've had are "under the spout where the glory comes out"—enjoying the abundant life with godly people I love. What are you going to hell for? Some overzealous or misinformed teacher or cleric or even a parent? The most important decision you will ever make—unquestionably—is getting right with God. *Today is the day of salvation.* Tomorrow is too late. Oh, sure, it may be too late if you die tonight. But the great truth is, once you know this joy, you too will ask why you waited even one more day to make your peace with God, change your mind about running your own life, and put it in God's loving hands. Here's a test: How often do you talk to Him?

Would you like to trust in God but you've listened to skeptics who question the historical validity of Christ or scripture? I'm afraid the skeptic's objections are obsolete. New discoveries continually affirm the entire treasury of scripture. Just consider the mathematical probability of 300 prophecies about Christ coming true, as they have. The probability that all these predictions could come true by natural means is so small that the mathematical calculation is staggering. You'd have to use 1 over 10 and some 84 zeroes.

God is love, and genuine love is the always answer to every problem. Even the vilest criminal wants to be treated with kindness—love.

Let's you and I talk about it.

For eye-popping answers to the questions you've always had, read *A Case for Faith*, by Lee Strobel, and *Divine Conspiracy*, by Dallas Willard.

I Had Blood On My Hands

Just as there are only two faiths in the world—worship of one God or self-worship—there are two choices on how to side with God: God's way or the human way. The human way—the wrong way—is to try to earn it, to "be good." Be honest. Haven't you acted or thought this way? Perhaps you've thought, "I need to get serious about spiritual things and my eternal destiny. I need to clean up my act. Then I can get right with God."

Major Grant Tyler, my boss at the Defense Information School, seemed to have his act together, but I detected something in what he said that set off alarms. I found it strange that he objected to a most entertaining and harmless promotion by a pirate!

"Captain Hook" had been a big, bad motorcycle gang member. He had turned his back on God, with whom he had a nodding acquaintance through the saintly life of his mother. But he wanted some so-called "fun," the kind that can thrill you and kill you. It almost did. He had a tragic accident and woke up in the hospital missing an arm and leg.

Recalling the counsel of his praying mother, he decided to trust Christ and felt a call on his life to reach kids for God. He went to seminary, met his beautiful wife, and built a ministry as a credible pirate with a believable "hook" and "wooden leg."

He headed a lovable and lighthearted cast of characters, all family, whom he named Mrs. Hook, Fish Hook and Cecil the Seasick Sea Serpent. Dressed in pirate costumes, they drove a bus through Grant Tyler's neighborhood, stopping and inviting kids to summertime fun at our church.

Grant thought it was terrible. I suppose under some bizarre circumstances I would agree with him, but his Methodist background would be compatible with the entertainment Captain Hook and his crew were brewing.

As a result, Grant and I got into a conversation about spiritual matters. I asked him what he'd answer if he died tonight and God queried him how he thought he would qualify for heaven.

Grant paused, and hesitatingly responded: "Kindness."

Alarms went off and I told him God requires something different than that. Kindness alone doesn't qualify. I thought I had plenty of time to convince him. I didn't.

Not long after that, Grant retired and went on a job search to support his lovely wife and two charming little girls. He failed to find a position commensurate with his style of living as a major.

He committed suicide.

God forgive me if I have Grant Tyler's blood on my hands. I failed to tell him what God Himself says would usher him into heaven:

For it is by grace you have been saved, through faith—and this not from yourselves, it is the gift of God—not by works, so that no one can boast (Ephesians 2: 8-9).

For the wages of sin is death, but the gift of God is eternal life in Christ Jesus our Lord (Romans 6:23, NIV).

That if you confess with your mouth, "Jesus is Lord," and believe in your heart that God raised him from the dead, you will be saved. For it is with your heart that you believe and are justified, and it is with your mouth that you confess and are saved (Romans 10:9-10, NIV).

> Martin Luther and millions of others discovered I can't earn my way to heaven. God's Word says it's a gift. Kindness before accepting and trusting in Christ becomes meaningless from an eternal point of view. Too many people have it backward. We all want kindness. But it must come from a transformed life. God takes over and empowers a soul to align with what God is doing in the world. That's what makes the difference, in a life, in the world. That is love. God is love.

Sign on church, attributed to God: "You catch 'em; I'll clean 'em."

Brook or Birds?

Dick and Margaret Patty had what I thought was a great job in Germany. They were missionaries to service members in the military and set up recreational retreats and seminars for those in the Armed Forces. They'd take soldiers or airmen, and government civilian employees, on ski weekends. In the evenings, Dick and Margaret would informally ask about life in the service or at home and they'd work the benefits of godly living into the conversation. Those who attended came back from the weekend outing relaxed and pumped, ready for the new week with renewed lives and vigor.

Margaret was a nurse, and sometimes she worked part-time for an Army medical facility. I recall hearing that one of the other missionary couples was having a tough time financially. Dick wasn't too concerned. He told of how God had performed some necessary work in his own family through finances—usually the lack of them. One time he told us an amazing story about God's provision of income.

He talked about the prophet Elijah having two sources of sustenance. He stayed by a brook for water and God sent ravens like clockwork, twice a day, to bring him food.

Dick applied the story to the situation in his own family. The ravens, he believed, were like friends back home who sent checks as part of their charitable giving. Of course, he didn't know how reliable that source of income would be, and as it happened, Margaret had an opportunity to work as a nurse for the Army. That would be a steady, reliable flow of income, just like Elijah's brook.

As it turned out, the charitable givers, like God's miraculous supply, kept up the flow of income. But as Dick found out about Elijah in 1 Kings 17, the brook dried up. In a budget cutback, the Army laid off Margaret. The Pattys' "brook" also dried up.

In that situation and in others, Dick said he learned much about how God supplies. Dick and Margaret were to work diligently, and put their faith in Jehovah Jirah, God the Provider, who never failed them in making sure the Pattys always had whatever they needed, right on time.

Heavenly Facial Changes

Hearing about that kid gripped me as few true stories ever have. Was his name Carl? Glen Cole told of his grandson, 5, who had a heart for the hurting. He'd go up to the altar and pray with people who knelt there for comfort or healing.

Glen Cole could preach powerfully. Suzanne and I heard him speak at two churches in Seattle, and he had a TV program for a while. We enjoyed his straight talk so much we decided to visit his church in Sacramento, on a 62-acre campus that featured a high school stadium with lights.

We had never seen such a church—6,500 seats, as I recall.

Glen told of Carl's overnight stay with them shortly after his great grandmother had died. Carl awoke when others were eating breakfast, and the little one rubbed his eyes and sat down.

"How was your sleep, Carl?"

"I dreamed about Grand-Mom and Jesus in heaven."

"Oh, my. That's nice. How was Grand-Mom?"

"She didn't look the same. She was much younger."

Everyone at the table looked at each other, first puzzled, and then nodding.

"And Jesus doesn't look like the pictures of him."

Interesting.

Some time later, the family was reading a scriptural passage in Revelation for their devotional time around the table.

And among the lampstands was someone "like a son of man," dressed in a robe reaching down to his feet and with a golden sash around his chest. His head and hair were white like wool, as white as snow, and his eyes were like blazing fire. His feet were like bronze glowing in a furnace, and his voice was like the sound of rushing waters. Revelation 1:13-15 (NIV)

"That's him!" Carl shouted, having intently listened.

"That's what Jesus looks like!"

I tell you the truth, anyone who will not receive the kingdom of God like a little child will never enter it.—Jesus, Luke 18:17 (NIV)

Upstaged

A little old lady stole the show at the traditional 8 a.m. service at Christ Memorial Church where Suzanne and I attend.

"In an average lifetime of 70 years, how many years does one sleep?" asked Pastor Tom Duchemin. Twenty-three years for most of us, according to a study.

"How long do we work?" Sixteen years was the answer.

"How much time do we spend in front of the TV?" Eight years.

"Eat?" Six. Same for travel.

"How much time are we ill?" Four years.

"How long do we spend at the doctor's?" Two years.

The next question got my attention, and the spontaneous answer from the congregation explains a lot.

"How much time do we spend in religious activity?"

The dear woman shouted it out from her pew.

"Seventy years!"

Pastor Tom had a tough time following that response.

"It's only zero-point-five," he said, sadly.

Tom made some adjustments in the second service to highlight the lady's wise response.

What transpired is why we have so many heartaches in the world. Too many people divide their lives into compartments. And for one or two hours on Sunday morning, they live in the compartment of religion. Even then, most of us, unfortunately, are thinking about what we're going to eat when the service is over.

The wise lady was correct. The person who takes the doors off his or her compartments and lives one's faith 24/7 is the person who finds true goodness and joy.

Tom's homily, fortunately, was aligned with the lady's concise but powerful sermon. He read a poem of one who would "rather see a sermon than hear one."

The sentiment matches the plaque on Army Chaplain McLaughlin's office wall in Heidelberg, Germany.

"Remember the Weekday, to Keep It Holy."

From Blasphemy to Awe

We had just finished talking about the royal official in John 4 who felt prompted to seek Jesus on behalf of his sick son. He took that first step, then acted on his faith, and his faith was affirmed and strengthened when he learned his son had recovered at the same moment Jesus said he was healed. The discussion took place at the Tuesday Bible study at the Corps of Engineers. We concluded how important it was to listen to the "still, small voice" of the Holy Spirit, respond to His promptings about little things, and He would entrust us with greater responsibility as we act in obedience.

On a gloomy morning I looked over at the glass of the bus shelter in the darkness. It was 4:40 a.m. There I saw stomach-turning blasphemy scrawled on the glass. I cannot ever repeat it. It was an unutterable and shameful verbal assault on God such that I had rarely seen before, even among godless people. I fought to push the filth from my mind.

"Clean it up!"

The Holy Spirit impressed upon me the need to rid the shelter of such abomination. But how? Was the message etched in the glass or written with some kind of permanent marker? I asked God to provide.

Previously I had remembered telling myself I must emphasize to the Bible study group that we need to make sure we respond to promptings that are aligned with God's Word and His will. I knew it was God's will to eradicate this verbal muck. Would He answer my prayer to provide the means? Surely He would. I prayed in accordance with His will.

Hastily I made up my mind to act. I thought I would need a cloth and water from a mud puddle. It had been raining frequently. I looked for the water I thought I needed. The street was bone-dry. Did I somehow miss my godly assignment? Attached to the shelter was a wastebasket. In it I found some newspaper. I recalled that newspaper did the best job cleaning my car windshields. No streaks. Despite having no water, I rubbed the vile words with dry newspaper. In a flash they totally disappeared without even a trace. It dawned on me that if I had found water from a puddle I would have smeared those windows with a muddy solution, not to mention ending up with shredded, sloppy handfuls of dirty paper. But now? Clean. Sparkling.

Suddenly that once dismal shelter became a cathedral. My spirit soared in gratitude, joy and worship. I sensed the awe of God's presence, and though I've disappointed Him many times, in that moment He made His message clear: "Well done, thou good and faithful servant." What a heavenly affirmation.

Now I can't wait. I am eager for my next assignment. But even more...I want to taste again the sweetness of that indescribably sacred encounter with God.

SITCOM

Daughter Tami is the one whom we call SITCOM—Single Income, Three Kids, Outrageous Mortgage.

The economists are all wrong. They don't understand God's economy. Tami's faithfulness to God has resulted in His amazing provision: three girls who are active in church, a well-paying job as a manager for Group Health Cooperative, her own home and the ability to buy a new car.

Those aren't the important things. The four of them flew to Wisconsin to be with the extended family at Christmas, and it has warmed our hearts to see the girls grow from mutual in-fighting to gradually appreciating one another's company.

I still remember some of granddaughter Jennifer's hilarious sayings when she was little. One time I was eating an orange and pulled out the white "tail" from inside with my teeth.

"Grandpa, you got the bone!"

"Sure! Look, I'll eat it, because it puts hair on my chest."

Tami told her, "You tell Grandpa you don't need that, because you're a girl."

"Grandpa," Jennifer scolded, "You don't eat oranges, because you're a girl."

OK, she sometimes got a bit confused.

Another time, when she was about 4, I was carrying her in my arms in a drugstore.

"Grandpa, Gracie's pregnant—very pregnant!"

"Gracie who?"

"You know, Grandpa. George and Gracie!"

"You know about George and Gracie Allen?"

"George and Gracie are the whales in Star Trek!"

It must run in the family. Her sister Kristen, among the others, went to our church on Palm Sunday.

"What did you learn in Sunday School, Kristen?"

"We saw a video of Jesus on a donkey and people throwing branches at him. He rode around for awhile and then saw some women and said, 'Hey, I'm with you!'"

"Are you sure that's what happened?"

"...I messed up."

Most of the adult infidels I know mess up when they discuss scripture with me or anyone within hearing. That's easy to do if one is arguing against the Bible they've never read. Reminds me of a story.

A co-called atheist says, "I can't believe those silly stories in the Bible."

"Oh? What story can't you believe?

"I just can't believe that Jonah swallowed a whale."

"Jonah swallowed a whale??? Where did you read that?"

"In the book of Genetics."

Yankee Morning—Thank You, Grandma Mac

Helen McMillin, my mother-in-law, seemed mildly interested in the spectacular sights of Seattle we showed her on her first trip out West to visit us from back home in Indiana.

On a drive through Discovery Park near Puget Sound, she spotted something that helped switch her vacation gears to that of a passion.

"Stop!" She saw a field of ripened, glistening blackberries. "You don't have to take me sightseeing anymore," she announced. "Just let me pick blackberries every day."

That she did. We enjoyed fresh blackberry cobbler until we couldn't move. Grandma Mac filled up our freezer, and those of all the neighbors, with countless plastic bags of blackberries.

Months later, Sister Kathy, husband Bob and family came home from Vermont, where Bob attended law school. I must have called him a Yankee, because he started one of his professorial lessons.

"When people in the South say 'Yankee,' they mean anyone up North," he said. "When someone in New York says 'Yankee,' they mean anyone in New England. When someone in New England says 'Yankee,' they mean anyone in Vermont. But when someone in Vermont says 'Yankee,' they mean someone who eats pie for breakfast."

We told him about Grandma Mac's freezers full of blackberries. Bob went out and bought us his favorite cookbook, *The Joy of Cooking*. Following it precisely, he meticulously made two blackberry pies, complete with crisscross crust on top.

The next morning we had hot blackberry pie for breakfast, with ice cream, of course, on top.

London's Culinary Arts

When I was assigned to Europe in the early 1980s, Suzanne and I invited her mother, Helen McMillin—Grandma Mac—along with our first granddaughter, Jennifer, and daughter Tami to visit us. We took a bus tour to London and saw Westminster Abbey, Buckingham Palace, the Crown Jewels, Trafalgar Square and all the sights.

The first day there I asked Grandma Mac where she'd like to eat. I suggested that there were all kinds of fish 'n chips places and quaint little pubs.

"Isn't that a Wendy's up ahead?" she asked. So we ate at Wendy's the first day.

The next day I said to Grandma Mac, "OK, we've eaten at Wendy's in London. Where should we eat today?"

She was quick to respond. "I saw a McDonald's back there," she volunteered.

The tour company offered some kind of tasteless buffet one evening, but that was about it. Wendy's and McDonald's.

Back in Germany, I told my friend, Mark Swearengen, and lamented the lack of variety we were obliged to consume on our tour, stuck with American franchise fast food.

Mark smiled. "In London, you can't do much better," he advised.

Alarm, Light and Remedy

When I told about the triumphs and tribulations of my Christian high school graduating class of 40 years, King's Class of 1962, Marge, in my adult Sunday School class became alarmed. My classmates love each other dearly, and most love the Lord, with several becoming medical staff, missionaries, teachers, non-profit workers and pastors, but the number is too large of those classmates who suffered divorces and disillusionment with "church-as-usual."

"How are we failing our Christian school students?" she asked. "What are Christian schools lacking in their teaching?" Enduring the pain of death by divorce myself, I've been troubled for years by those questions.

Shame on me. I really had no expectation that the small-town pastor in a remote Wisconsin church would turn the light on for me as no one else had in my 57 years. Rev. Dean Anderson pastors a vibrant church near Wisconsin Rapids, where son Mike and his wife Polly live with Austin, then 4, and Brenna, who was 1.

Listen carefully. Dean's words explain much that's going on in and out of the church world: "Biblical principles without Biblical thinking leads to short-term obedience and long-term frustration." Out of the blue, he had put his finger on a profound truth. That's it! Going through the motions, no matter how sincerely, won't cut it. Sooner or later, without a deeper understanding of the reasons behind scriptural teaching, we give in to temptation and chances are, we give up on Christ's promise of living life abundantly as He said. Without that understanding, the life of faith looks like a long list of "don'ts" and killjoy rules. Nothing could be further from the truth. The vibrant life of joy Christ was talking about results from partnering with Him to get the upper hand on self-defeating habits that eventually trip us up and land us in a ditch of depression and moral failure.

Instead, as Bruce Wilkinson simply points out in *Secrets of the Vine*, one has a phenomenal opportunity to be grafted into Christ Himself, tapping into unspeakable power to produce an overflowing basket of fruit that benefits others as it fulfills oneself. And as Dallas Willard says in *Divine Conspiracy*, my generation and younger have been spoiled by the fast-food variety of religion. Go to the

133

altar and find instant transformation. That's not the usual pattern in scripture. It's a lifelong growth process involving spiritual disciplines. One who thinks he or she can master a rewarding life without the disciplines is cruising to failure. Willard names some of classics, along with the downside and upside: "There has been abuse and misunderstanding, no doubt, but the power of solitude, silence, meditative study, prayer, sacrificial giving, service, and so forth as disciplines are simply beyond question....we remain ignorant of it to our great disadvantage." He says these disciplines, developed into habits, result in a fulfillment of Christ's promise that His yoke is easy and His burden is light. I never understood that before.

I have concluded from these gentlemen's teachings that three factors may have caused some of my classmates and me to stumble along the way: we didn't heed the "why" behind the timeless principles, merely going through the motions; we sought instant transformation at the altar instead of a lifetime of joy-producing habitual discipline; and we struggled with man-made rules disguised as God's, as Jesus accused the Pharisees. Failing, some of us may have turned our backs on God and given up. Josh McDowell finds three scriptural reasons for this rejection in *Evidence That Demands a Verdict*: ignorance, pride and/or a moral problem. Buddy Gene Neudigate tells of a pastor whose preacher-dad ran off with another woman. Struggling through poverty with his mother and siblings for a period in his life, the son-pastor reported, gladly, that his dad had repented—turned from his sin. "But the damage had already been done." Yet, the son's suffering resulted in a triumphant ministry by one who understood the pain of his parishioners. I am reminded of a woman weaving a beautiful Persian rug. A visitor asked what happened if she made a mistake. "The Creative Designer makes the flaw part of the final pattern and transforms it into a masterful work of art."

I feel a periodic tug toward my old Christian high school. I would be humbled if somehow, someday, I might fill in the rest of the story for today's young students, thanks to the incisive teaching of men of God like Dean Anderson. Meanwhile, may God enable me to communicate and demonstrate his message to my six granddaughters, a message best caught, not taught.

Coach's Far-Sighted Vision

Dwight Nyquist was a breath of fresh air at King's Garden High School. Languishing in sports mediocrity, the athletes and would-be athletes found their spirits soaring when this Wheaton College All Conference football great came to coach their teams.

Coach Nyquist, in his mid-twenties, brought energy, wit and fresh blood to the sports outlook. This had been a bedraggled program where penniless boys dug through a box to find used football boots to wear, and years later, tough-and-tender Dave Stump shed tears when he told a football reunion how one coach had given his meager missionary salary to help outfit the young Stump who had no other resources.

As one of the successor coaches, Dwight had already served two years in the Army and now was giving another two years to this low-paying Christian endeavor. "Every person should give at least two years of his life to his country and two or more years to God." He was a good-looking blond who spoke at chapels and beach bonfires, with every student eagerly soaking in his every word.

Conducting a summer football camp at the campus, which hosted students and players in dormitories, Dwight taught discipline and perseverance. At least once a day, the football hopefuls would fall out to the "rock garden"—a plot of ground where he hoped that the football team would someday play. But now it was a field of dirt and more rocks than you could count. The players spent an hour a day picking up countless stones. They would practice over yonder and play the real games under the lights at nearby Hamblin Park.

Despite the inspiration—Dwight would lead his team in singing, "On the Field He is My Captain…no turning back, no turning back"—despite the discipline, despite new uniforms, despite hardy team training meals, despite a veteran coaching staff—the win-loss football record during those two years was somewhat disappointing. We learned character in defeat, while the Stump boys, Dan Koser, Byron Woolsey and others provided individual battlefield combat against their helmeted foes week after week.

Dwight's dream was for us to play on that rock garden. He envisioned a lush, green field, spectacular under the lights. He contacted a candy company and dispatched scores of students selling candy door-to-door to raise funds for those lights.

His two-year quest was exhausting. He moonlighted at Seattle Pacific College to help feed his growing family. He quipped that "King's provides my bread and butter; Seattle Pacific provides my meat and potatoes." If I recall correctly, the "missionary" salary for teachers at King's was $40 a month, plus room and board, for singles; $120 and housing for married staff. Struggling to make ends meet, Dwight chose to find employment with Shoreline Community College. Though we looked up to him as mentor and champion, he left, fieldwork undone, but having inspired dozens of boys to persevere and create solutions despite adversity.

A quarter century later, King's had a special Homecoming for former players and coaches. I climbed to the top row of the new bleachers to watch a talented King's football team in a downpour. A former coach and his wife came up and happened to sit in the row in front of me. It was Dwight and his wife Lorraine! We were dry, under a sturdy roof that covered the glistening aluminum seating, looking down on a luxuriant green field.

I leaned forward and whispered, "Coach, you started it all. Your candy sales launched the vision for this night-lighted stadium."

Lorraine eyes opened wide. "You remember that?"

All of Dwight's blood, sweat and tears had finally culminated in a magnificent facility that was the pride of students, players, coaches, faculty and alumni.

Woolsey Field is truly a wonder to behold. Imagining seeing that expansive sight through Dwight's eyes, I couldn't help but think that God reminded the old coach of His field operations plan:

The man who plants and the man who waters have one purpose, and each will be rewarded according to his own labor.
(I Corinthians 3:8, NIV)

Being confident of this, that he who began a good work in you will carry it on to completion until the day of Christ Jesus. (Philippians 1:8, NIV)

Postscript: I asked Dwight to read this before I published it. In his uniquely humble way, he said, "I was so honored just to be listed as an All-Conference player. When I think of the good buddies who blocked and tackled with equal if not surpassing effort, I realize how unfair it is to single out any one player when it takes a 'team' to win. The stadium at King's is a perfect example. It is the 'rock pickers' and 'candy salespersons' that are the real heroes."

My Mark in the World

Buddy Dan and I had great fun staying in the dorm at King's Garden and delivering food all over campus. And I do mean all over.

King's—now also called Crista—had a 42-acre campus—bigger now—that included schools, a printing press, radio stations, apartments and a rest home. Steam tunnels connected a number of the buildings. Dan and I would load a cart with steam kettles full of hot food. We'd roll the cart onto a freight elevator and ride the cart through the darkened concrete tunnels to the awaiting hungry senior citizens. Sometimes, through no fault of our own, the food was late. Those dear old souls patiently sat at the long tables singing hymns.

The tunnels were built at angles, so we had to steer carefully to negotiate the turns. A few times velocity (we learned this in Mr. Mills' physics class) and inertia caused us to, well, lose control.

Twenty-five years after I graduated I was looking in a display case at King's for a glimpse of trophies our class had won. I spotted a couple that even had my name on them, but they were half buried and covered with dust. On the next visit they had been moved. I doubt if I'll see them again.

But I know the mark Dan and I made in 1961 still graces the walls of those steam tunnels. It's that glob of spinach that spilled over the side going around that last curve.

Higher Education—
A Less Enjoyable Introduction
to Adult Life

My two years at Seattle Pacific College should have been the best of my life, but after three incomparable years at King's, SPC turned out to be something of a letdown, or at least a reality check. In retrospect, I may have tapped into campus life more had I stayed in the dorm instead of at home. In fact, if I were to do it all over again, I would have grown up faster if I borrowed the money and attended Wheaton College or a place like Azusa Pacific University.

SPC was good for a few laughs, despite its rather stuffy academic atmosphere. The college named buildings after former presidents of the institution—Marston, Peterson, Watson. One of the oldest buildings was Alexander Hall. Was there a President Alexander? No, this Free Methodist school dared not name a building Beers Hall after Alexander Beers!

To earn tuition, I dug ditches, struggled with maintenance duties and scrubbed toilets, floors and dishes. Buddy Dan Koser and I would feed dishes onto the moving conveyor sprocketed belt into the scalding hot dishwasher. About six young women stood by another conveyor belt. Each would leisurely take glassware, plate or silverware off the belt and place the one or two items onto a tray overhead.

One day the administration held an award ceremony in the Commons. The young women left their post to watch the proceedings, but the dirty food trays full of dishes kept coming along the belt. Dan and I rushed to pull everything off onto the overhead trays, and then we ran the dishes through the dishwasher.

The lady boss watched. Apparently burdened by high student labor costs, she approached Dan and me. "How would you two like to take over the whole operation—conveyor belt, trays, dishwasher, all of it, seven days a week, three meals a day, 40 hours a week?"

We agreed. We could use the money, and even though it meant horrendous shifts morning noon and night, along with full academic loads, we took it on.

Our grades suffered, and I used to fall asleep dangling over my bed studying zoology, but it taught us much about work efficiency at $1.25 an hour. Well, except for that time I wanted to ride through the dishwasher and look at the plumbing just for fun. I carefully turned off the water for the adventure. Half way through, Dan opened the valves to the scalding hot water. My egress was like that circus fella shot out of a cannon.

But, what are friends for, anyway?

Small World and a High-Priced Education

I keep running into people with connections to my past. Jonathan Maas at the Corps is an environmental restoration guy. He lived two doors down from me in sixth grade and he used to beat me up. Now I'm bigger than he is, and he's more respectful.

The Corps' Dale Bryant knew all my kindergarten playmates and had the same teachers in Des Moines, south of Seattle.

Cindy Wikstrom at the Corps knew my folks and siblings. She's the one who brought her Uncle Winston, my organist hero and camp counselor, to the Corps Centennial.

Daughter Julie and son Gary had their connections as well. They always had more than their share of friends. Dad called Gary "Six Arms" because he was always so busy. Julie got involved in gymnastics, drama and music, as did her big brother.

I remember a feature showing some men, involved with an Eastern religion, sitting cross-legged and hovering about 6 inches off the floor in a still picture. Turns out that they "hopped" for the picture, creating the illusion of hovering. I have a picture of Julie, upside down, "hovering" above the ground. I snapped her picture as she performed a gymnastic flip.

Gary and Julie enjoyed performing in musicals in their high school in Seattle while Suzanne, Mike and I were in Europe. When we returned to the States and settled down in Seattle, Gary and Julie took me for a ride around the city.

I was having a tough time adapting to my new job at the Corps of Engineers. The boss who hired me, Colonel Roger Yankoupe, had the reputation of expecting late hours and had a harsh, "old-school" management style that made my intestine occasionally seize up when he spoke to me! He lived with his family in a historic home at the locks in the Seattle community of Ballard. The Corps built and operates the locks.

Cruising around the city, Gary and Julie suggested we go see their school chum, Ruthie. Ruthie worked at the famous Totem Fish and Chips place across from the locks. We talked with Ruthie and I mentioned we had just returned from Germany.

"Oh, I lived in Germany with my family," she said. "My dad was an Army officer in Europe."

"Yeah," Gary said. "Her dad and family live right over there in that house at the locks."

I gulped. "Who is your dad, Ruthie?"

"Colonel Roger Yankoupe."

O my. Colonel Yankoupe later was to get his jollies by playing on people's fears. Learning that Equal Employment Officer Julio Garcia was afraid of heights and helicopters, the colonel ordered a chopper with Vietnam-trained pilots to take the colonel, Julio and a couple other managers to Wynoochee Dam. The colonel had instructed the pilots not to descend gradually into the dam, but to shut off the engine at high altitude and auto-rotate into the dam property. Horrified, Julio screamed all the way down, certain he was about to die. Just before impact, the pilot restarted the engine and landed safely. Julio had wet his pants. The other managers restrained his fisticuffs as the colonel laughed with delight.

Let's just say that Gary and Julie's schoolmate's father gave me a million-dollar education I wouldn't pay a dime to repeat.

Moral Victory

Son Mike and pal Jon Neudigate played their hearts out in junior high basketball. They had dreams of playing at higher levels. Once benched for poor grades, Mike studied harder than ever and successfully avoided a repeat.

Jon's dad, Gene, knew the game better than most, having starred in high school as one of Indianapolis' top five players. One day he turned to me at one of our sons' junior high games and told me that both boys were good players, but because of the talent coming up from cross-town Clay Junior High, our boys likely wouldn't see action as high school players.

Shortly thereafter, I landed a job in Heidelberg, Germany. Mike was sixth player on the team at the Heidelberg American High School, a team that became the European Champions. Organizers selected Mike to play on a team that was to play in a French tournament with teams from all over Europe, from as far away as Yugoslavia. He said sometimes his team slept in the locker room next to members of the opposing teams.

"It stank," he said. "They didn't know about deodorant."

Mike was surprised at the French welcome. The team mounted a platform on the floor below the gymnasium, and the platform rose to come into sight of the throngs above, with spotlights and pageantry. The French crowd cheered for the Americans throughout the two days of games.

After two years in Europe, we came home to Seattle and began "shopping" for a good basketball school for Mike. Someone suggested I call my old Alma Mater, King's.

"When I was there, they couldn't play their way out of a paper bag," I said, but I gave Coach Larry Skogstad a call.

"I don't want to brag," Larry said, "but I'm the winningest coach in the state," he said. "We haven't lost a league game for eight years."

Without further hesitation, we enrolled Mike at King's. Before basketball season started, a rumor circulated among his classmates that a German student had enrolled in order to play basketball.

Mike started as senior point guard and his team went to state finals at the Tacoma Dome. Several colleges called him, and he was invited to try out by an assistant coach at Seattle Pacific University, where I attended.

"We'd like you to be part of the team," the SPU coach told him, "but we're saving our scholarship money for the tall kids." Mike is 6-foot-zero. Hearing that, he skipped the tryout.

We had attended Aurora Church of the Nazarene, who offered a small scholarship to Nazarene kids who went to Northwest Nazarene College. NNC sponsored an activities day in Nampa, Idaho, to enable high school students to see the campus and to compete in games. The NNC coach watched Mike play and offered him a partial scholarship.

The scrappy Mike spent much of his playing time falling on the floor, causing an opposing player to commit a charging foul. Our son ended up starting four seasons.

It wasn't until his senior year that Seattle Pacific appeared on the schedule. NNC would play SPU in Seattle. I bought 23 tickets and brought half the church to the game.

Mike's team led the host team at half time. SPU's coach heatedly chided his superior team for letting Idaho's little-known school beat them. Throughout the second half, Mike continued to play with all his heart.

SPU squeaked out a victory. Was this a defeat? Not on your life.

Mike scored his career high.

We relished every one of Mike's 25 points against the school that was stingy with the scholarship money. His school had fewer overall points, but we went home feeling nothing but triumph—sweet victory.

Accused of Child Abuse

How could it possibly be?

"Billy said you hit him!"

My wife, Suzanne, would be charged with child abuse at the pre-school where she worked. The administration put her on paid suspension.

It didn't matter that Suzanne never hit any child, that the school didn't allow capital punishment nor that every staff member must be in view of another.

"My child never lies," Billy's mother had told the principal. Never mind that she previously had told staff members she had caught Billy in a number of lies.

Even so, Suzanne now faced a panel made up of representatives from the police department and child protective service.

A police officer questioned Suzanne. As it turned out, he was a fellow believer. He asked her if Billy had any friends at school.

"He plays a lot with Freddie," she replied.

"Freddie who?

We know his parents. His Mom works in the department. I'll have her bring him over.

Soon the little buddy entered the room. Seeing Suzanne, his face lit up, and he flew across the room to give Suzanne a hug.

"Mrs. Harris! What are *you* doing here?"

The police officer got him settled and gave him drawing paper and crayons.

"Freddie, did you ever see anyone hit Mrs. Harris?"

"No-o-o," he said confidently with a smile of disbelief, as if the questioner were joking.

Then, the climactic question.

"Freddie, did you ever see Mrs. Harris hit anyone?

Who could have foreseen the impenetrable network of saints and angels God had placed in that room, interconnected, so that the questioner had known even the pre-kindergarten surprise witness. Again, Freddie's mouth broke into a smile. His eyes sparkled.

"Aaaaah-so-loooot-lee *not*!

The littlest angel had retrieved the grownup expressions from some tiny crevice in his developing mind.

"We have no case here," the police officer said, and the panel agreed.

What a relief to Suzanne. They were comforting words, but they didn't begin to compare with the words of a little boy.

No orator had ever uttered such eloquence.

Kitty Littercycle

Buying a used Honda 360 motorcycle was one of my biggest mistakes.

Both spills occurred at low speeds. The first happened at work in Indianapolis coming to a stop in the rain. Nobody instructed me that braking in the rain can cause spills if you let the wet back wheel keep going while you try to stop the front wheel. No big deal. Putting it down only wounded my pride.

I bought yellow slicker rain jacket and pants. Would they keep me dry? No. Without proper boots, the rain outfit efficiently funneled water into my shoes.

I motorcycled back and forth to Gruesome, er, Grissom Air Force Base for reserve duty. One duty day I remembered that reservists (at that time) could use the commissary once a year. Now we can use it anytime we want. But with an average savings of about 28 percent on groceries, I would not let the opportunity pass. I bought several bags full of groceries, and a large sack of kitty litter.

"You're a reservist, aren't you?" The cashier had me pegged.

"How did you know?"

"I can spot 'em a mile away," she said. "You're buying 12 tubes of Head 'n Shoulders shampoo to last you for the rest of the year."

Putting the bags in a cart, I walked outside to the parking lot.

"Oh, no!"

I'd spaced out. You don't go to the commissary when you're riding a motorcycle. I tried to make the best of it. I stuffed bags in my blue Air Force windbreaker and secured the kitty litter and my briefcase on the back rack. How do you steer when you feel like you have Santa's toy sack pressing down on your belly? I reached around the huge bulge the best I could.

I remembered someone telling Pastor Tom Bell, "Dave must have guardian angels riding with him, or he'd be dead by now."

"He's got Jesus Himself riding with him," Tom responded.

"Dave, you'd better let Jesus get off—you're going to kill him."

The briefcase made several attempts to jump off the back. I ended up carrying it with my left hand and steering with my right. After riding 55 miles, about five miles from home, shampoo and everything else tried again and again to escape the torn bags. I juggled the load in front.

146

I became puzzled. Why did the highway behind me appear a light gray from my rear view mirror?

Simple. When kitty absorbent granules flow freely from a torn bag, they litterally change the color of the landscape. Nuts.

Several weeks later, son Mike was riding on the back, dutifully helmeted. I was going maybe 5 miles per hour, coming to a stop, when I hit some sand. Over we went. Mike went into convulsions, and I got a nasty gash on my ankle. Fortunately a nurse saw what happened and attended to Mike, leaving me to limp home on that crummy machine.

I got rid of that deathtrap soon after. I rode it only one more time—at the farm of the new owner, "Uncle Joe," around the edge of his pond.

Suzanne still wonders why I didn't drown.

Fuzzy Ice Cream Ritual

Religion that God our Father accepts as pure and faultless is this: to look after orphans and widows in their distress and to keep oneself from being polluted by the world. James 1:27 (NIV)

Gwen Postma was a tiny woman, suffering from lifelong spinal problems, but as our typing teacher she was full of sunshine and laughter. Her only son, Loren, had a Willies Jeepster, and Dan and I hung around with him.

We weren't orphans, but we almost wish we were, because of the great treatment they got from Gwen. She would invite orphans from school home with her for as long as necessary, and she'd invite Dan and me over for the night as well. The Postma family lived in a little farmhouse in Kirkland, Wash., complete with goats and ducks and chickens. We thought it was Paradise.

Gwen and her husband, Posty, always had a half-dozen flavors of ice cream in the freezer, and we enjoyed a bowl every time we went over there.

Perhaps 30 years after we graduated from high school, Dan and I decided to drop in on the Postmas. Gwen finally retired, teaching at King's for a couple decades after we graduated. The visit was just as if we had never left. Gwen and Posty would both pray simultaneously and out loud over a meal. When Loren was there, he'd try to tickle his dad during the prayer. What fun—here were two prayers going at the same time, long, deep and sincere, confusing for the competition, and lengthened even more as Posty would interrupt his with an occasional giggle.

During our nostalgic visit, we reminisced about the freezer full of ice cream. "Oh, we still have a lot of that," Posty said with delight. "Go downstairs and bring up a few cartons. You can finish them up!"

We came back with armfuls of cartons. We opened them up and most of them had freezer-burn fuzz inside. The ice cream ritual was too much a part of our visits to let that stop us. We loaded our bowls up with the stale stuff and enjoyed the cold, sweet dregs.

Every time we see Loren or Posty—Gwen finally went home to the Lord—they ask us, "Wanna come home and have some fuzzy ice cream?!"

Every Message for Me

Classmate Heather Lush Duffy taught me a lesson that will last for the rest of my life. I overheard her telling others about it during the King's High School Class of 1962 25th Reunion in 1987.

She had decided to take every spiritual lesson—from books, sermons or articles—as a message from God intended specifically for her. I found this to be such a phenomenal idea, and it has helped me focus on great messages when I might otherwise be daydreaming about Starbucks Java Chip ice cream. I must admit, however, that I haven't always practiced Heather's brilliant lesson.

But I was impressed with an example of how Heather practiced her intent.

One Sunday evening she stopped in at church for the evening service. The pastor spoke of the importance of following Christ's example in baptism. It didn't occur to Heather that this particular sermon applied to her, and she began to drive home.

Suddenly she remembered her intent to regard every spiritual lesson as shaped especially for her. She turned the car around, and drove back to the church.

After telling the pastor her intended practice, she soon resumed her drive home, but not before taking care of business.

Her hair was wet. True to her resolution, she had been immersed in the baptismal waters that very night.

2 Sermons for the Price of 1

Li-Shine Lin, a Taiwanese American, came into my office to interview for the position of clerk-typist. As I looked through her application, my mouth watered: former owner of "Egg Rolls to Go" restaurant, one degree in nutrition—she had earned a master's degree…reading the application and listening to her made me hungry, so I hired her, of course. She has a beautiful home and three children. I ended up hiring a daughter, Janice, after Li-Shine moved up to a better job. Li-Shine has invited the whole office and spouses over for lavish Chinese dinners and brings me Asian goodies from time to time.

Suzanne and I have visited her church on a couple occasions. When the church was looking for a permanent pastor, Li-Shine asked me if I would be willing to speak to the congregation some Sunday morning. The service was all in Taiwanese, and she would translate.

She asked me for some notes so she could prepare. My notes were rather sketchy. The big morning arrived, and "Mr. Ray" greeted me. He said Li-Shine was unable to attend that morning and he would translate.

I began the sermon and spoke a sentence at a time, waiting for Mr. Ray to translate. We continued for about 20 minutes that way. I concluded my remarks on a rather serious note. Mr. Ray followed up. Suddenly the congregation roared in laughter. I was puzzled. I didn't remember saying anything lighthearted or odd at that point.

Afterwards, I asked Mr. Ray what I said that made people laugh.

"Oh, no, it wasn't you," he said. I had some trouble expressing in Taiwanese some of the things you had said during your talk. So I told them, 'Today you heard two fine sermons. One from Mr. Harris, and the other from me!'"

Women's Pendulum Swing

How many classes have you sat through that you remember them for the rest of your life? I think this one was called, "How to deal with difficult people."

The instructor was gray-haired and close to retirement. We'll call her Maggie. She had a few minutes at the end of her lesson, so she let down her hair and told us of one of her insightful observations.

"Back in the 1970s," she said, "women signed up in droves for assertiveness training. I have no problem with assertiveness. That simply means putting everything on the table and addressing it rationally."

So far, so good.

"But that behavioral change was like the pendulum swinging 45 degrees to the left. If that's where it ended up all would be well."

What was bothering her?

"But the pendulum swung too far beyond that—all the way to aggressive."

Oh-oh.

"Now, women are realizing they went too far in that direction, and most are working their way back on the pendulum—back to assertive."

Makes sense to me. We can think of a few guys that would do well to follow suit.

Under the Spout Where the Glory Runs Out

Rising daily at 3:40 a.m. to catch the ferry, I've never slept in. Or rarely. If I go to California or Wisconsin to visit loved ones on an extended vacation, I still awaken at 4, 5 or 6—that's sleeping in for me.

The same happened at a churchmen's retreat at Island Lake on the Kitsap Peninsula. Beautiful place, but I don't think I'll ever go to an overnight open-bay event again. In the first place I snore. My red-eyed roommates try to be nice about it, but one can practically lose one's salvation struggling to sleep in the same room as I. So I don't sleep very well at a retreat anyway. I worry that I'll sound like a foghorn.

I woke up around 5 that Saturday morning. With maybe a dozen or so guys in the cabin, I became concerned that the hot water wouldn't last for everyone to take a shower. I decided to take mine while the others slept.

I've never operated strange showers very well. Sometimes I'd run the water waiting for it to get hot, and I'd turn it the wrong way. This shower was odd. The faucet was rather loose. I got in. The water was lukewarm. I kept turning the faucet around and around, trying to get more hot water.

Imagine this: You're naked. Twelve people are asleep within 20 feet of you. You're quietly trying to take an innocent shower. Suddenly the faucet falls off. A 2-inch geyser of water loudly gushes, shooting straight out, past you, past the shower curtain, inundating the wall across from the shower stall, where the towels are hanging.

You stoop over, pick up the faucet, and try to push it back in. You fail.

I grabbed a towel, and ran into the sleeping room.

"Hey guys! Sorry to ruin your sleep, but the shower broke and water is shooting out!"

Where's my video camera when I need it? Suddenly chaos broke out. Someone shouted, "Find the shut-off valve outside!" Everyone ran around in their underwear. Three guys ran out in the morning light in their skivvies looking for the valve. Nowhere in sight.

152

You discover an interesting variety of personalities in such a situation. Some people watch in disbelief. Some try to take charge, but they have no idea what to do. I was impressed by a quiet but determined leader-type who simply stripped, grabbed the detached faucet and forced it back into the gushing hole, turning it until he solved the problem.

All was finally quiet and wet—the most heart-pounding baptism in which I had ever participated.

Perhaps it was a sign from God. Stay away from retreats and give the other guys some rest.

I was thankful it was the worst crisis I had to face that decade. I am a blest man.

Epilogue: I told this story to Suzanne. She asked who the hero repairman was.

"I never met him before, and I haven't seen him since," I said. "Maybe he was an angel."

"No," she retorted. "I think after that he changed religions."

Auto Boomerang

All four Harris siblings have been involved in overseas missionary endeavors. The Air Force enabled me to participate in building a home for orphaned boys in Korea. Brother Thom and his wife, Ardyce, traveled to Poland and their daughter, Keisha, served in Tibet. Sister Kathy and her husband, Bob, and family have served many years in China. Sister Laurie and husband, John, and family served nine months in Albania.

Before departure to Albania, John and Laurie offered their Toyota Camry to Mom to drive while they were gone. One day she went to the back parking lot at her apartment complex, and the car was gone. We notified the police, as well as John and Laurie. We were concerned that a cell phone was in the trunk. The police said there had been several incidents and suspected someone who may have had too many drinks at the bar on the main highway a block above Mom's place.

Mom had previously sold her car and had gotten used to taking the bus most places she went. But she had looked forward to using the Camry, because she loved to go "garage sailing." She often found bargain antiques and developed an expertise for determining their value and selling them on consignment at "The Cat's Meow," an antique boutique in which several vendors displayed their wares.

A couple weeks went by, and we lost hope that the police would find the stolen car, despite our prayers.

Yet another week passed, and Mom hiked a block to the Poulsbo Market to pick up a few groceries. When she emerged, she noticed a car that looked a bit like the lost Camry. She walked closer. Surely it wasn't. It was!

Call the police. They wouldn't let her drive it home just yet. They staked out the store, hoping to catch the thief coming out to drive it away. No one turned up.

Could it be that Mom had left it there weeks before and forgot about it?

No, the police said. They patrol the parking lot often.

I e-mailed Laurie and John of the incredible news.

In their Albanian home, they read the message.

Looked at each other.

154

Read it again.

Looked at each other.

Disbelieving, they grabbed the phone.

"Yes, it's true."

So many people have told me, "Dave, we never know when you're serious."

Sometimes I'll start a story like the late Steve Allen: "All seriousness aside…"

But when it comes to reappearing cars, I kid you not.

Reciprocal Puttering

Dad took brother Thom and me on his remodeling and electronic door opener service calls. Nothing seemed to stump Dad, be it mechanical, electrical, plumbing, whatever. Thom paid attention. I didn't. To me, those service calls were always too wet, too cold, too boring, and too dark. So, as buddy Gene Neudigate says, he and I have the mechanical ability of a walnut. Or walrus. Suzanne must put together desks and entertainment centers needing assembly. It's not that I haven't tried. I've just learned over the years that I'm money ahead if I see if someone else can fix or assemble things. When buddy Dan Koser or brother Thom comes over, they are more than happy to fix a window or repair a clock, and I'm delighted to let them.

One day, however, I thought I could take on the ceiling fan that wasn't running. I could handle changing a switch. I installed a wall switch of the same type from downstairs. I knew that was working. No success. I started sweating. Gene and Colette were visiting, and Gene tried to assist. Dead in the water. Check the circuit breakers. Everything's in order. So, I unscrewed the ceiling fan. It dangled there for weeks. Nothing inside, anyway, looked out of place. Call Warren, sister Laurie's father-in-law. He came over with an electrical meter and detected a tiny amount of current, but not enough. Stumped.

Finally, daughter Tami's brother-in-law, Todd, came over. Todd's a pretty good handy man. He told me it would be easier to re-wire all the way from the circuit box to the ceiling fan by stringing wire through the attic. He crawled up there and surveyed the job, then came right back down.

"Dave, come over here," he said quietly. "What's this switch for?" He showed me a switch in the foyer next to the family room where the ceiling fan is. That switch was turned off and shared duties with the suspect switch. How embarrassing. I could have restored the ceiling fan just by turning on the other switch! To make me feel better, Todd told me he could re-connect the switches properly so they could be operated independently.

I have just one redeeming social value, however. I can program video tape recorders and TVs. Visiting Dan, I found that he had a newer Sony TV that cycled through only from channels 2 to 13, even though the cable company fed some 100 channels into his home. I pushed a button and the TV "found" the other 87 channels.

So, let's barter. You fix my car, my desk, my dryer, my faucet, my door, my lock, my window, my clock, my bookshelf, my water heater. I'll come over and see that you can watch TV. Such a deal.

Skinny Chapter; Skinny Results?

All my life I've been too skinny or too fat.

The folks offered me a dollar for every pound I could gain when I was 7. I was a "weak-side guard" in high school football—too light for my violent endeavor. Weak? What a lousy name for a football position. I think I was all of 120 pounds. I may have said I was 150 and the football program said 165. They added the 15 pounds of the uniform.

Marriage did me in. Those sack lunches with candy bars and snowball cupcakes started building their lodging place around my middle. The Air Force insisted I stay under 199 pounds, but I think I overhung that by 10 or 15 pounds. When my legs and back gave me problems around age 28, I took up jogging. Ultimately I ran several 15-milers and the Indy 500 Mini-Marathon.

All the running didn't cure my weight problem. After a good workout, I'd load up with ice cream. When I retired from the Air Force Reserve, I ballooned up to 245. *The Weigh Down Diet* helped me shed 57 pounds and keep much of it off for a couple years. I could eat anything I wanted—but only when genuinely hungry and then I ate only half a portion. But winning the battle for the long haul—it's a lifelong skirmish.

A celebrity who shed 80 pounds or so said he did it by taking the best from all the many diets he had ever tried. That's it! So, here it is—the advice of all the gurus. Follow these top 10 tips, and your victory over weight—and keeping it off—is assured:

10. Delay your food intake—when you feel mildly hungry, delay munching by drinking water or a non-sugar soft drink. One advisor says not to drink a diet drink until you first drink a glass of water. No pressing need to drink as many as eight or more glasses for weight loss, but healthy amounts of plain water helps prevent kidney stones.

9. Put your fork down between bites. Double or triple the time you expend to take a bite and chew your food. The slower you eat, the more accurately your stomach sends "full" signals. Caution: the "full" signal is broken for some like me. Focus on the time more than the signal.

8. Cut down on sugar, breads and other starches—carbohydrates release insulin, converting sugar to fat. The "fat-free" label on cookies and candy is a scam. See how much sugar the product offers.

7. If you take in any modest amount of sugar or starch, skip the stuff after 3 p.m.

6. Divide your exercise in thirds—15 to 20 minutes, three times a day, five times a week. My favorite: a mini-tramp, while watching TV or a video.

5. Add moderate weightlifting to your aerobics—start light and add weight until 10-20 reps make you too tired to continue without a short rest.

4. After your brief rest—5 minutes—do another set of reps, a second rest and a third set.

3. Cross-training—Do two or three kinds of aerobic exercise each week: tramp, walk, jog, tennis, racquetball, bike. Swimming is good for other things, but not so hot for weight loss.

2. Wind-sprints—in the middle of your aerobics routine, do a minute or more with strenuous speed. However, most of your session should be slow enough so you can talk without huffing and puffing.

And, if all else fails, the Number One tip that, practiced with the others, assures your weight loss:

1. Write down every food or drink you put into your mouth.

Oops! I just got on the scale. Forget everything after "Hello."

The Last Word,
or What I Didn't Say

I did it again. I kept my mouth shut. Sometimes that's good, but I had rehearsed my speech for the next time my new next-door neighbor called my president "Shrub." I was going to say that I joined federal service under Lyndon Johnson and faithfully carried out the policies of presidents no matter who was in office, and I intended to support President Bush as well.

I chickened out. But in John's favor, he put down presidents of any party. In fact, John puts down just about everything.

O my. All the things we intended to say, or thought of later. Like telling off the boss. Or rather than get ourselves in trouble, we wish we'd have thought of some disarming, clever quip that settled the whole matter, once and for all.

But do I have to win every argument? Lots of things are left unsaid. Yet, there's one thing I thought of later I wish I had said. I ride one of the earliest ferries often when it's still dark to sail to my Seattle job. I sat down at an empty table, on an empty bench, across from another empty bench. Two empty tables down, a lone passenger said, "You can't sit there. That's for the regulars."

Fortunately, one of the "regulars" was good enough to smooth things over, and she told me I could stay seated, and that they would sit "over there."

Ever since, I think of what I could have said: "You know, Sir, I have been riding this ferry since 1948. I have provided the revenue for this whole vessel and all its furnishings. You are welcome to share it with me."

Best left unsaid?

The ferryboat has its intricate unwritten etiquette. I stand in line at the front, well before docking, so I can run and get a seat on the bus. Etiquette: If you leave more than 18 inches between you and the person in front of you, someone else is welcome to step in front of you and take your place. Keep my mouth shut! By the way, that 18-inch standard went for width of butts, too. The ferries were designed for estimated but width, causing much heartache and overcrowding, butt I'm not going to talk about that either.

In the afternoon, I often walk around the top deck, doing laps for 20-30 minutes. The newer ferries have a narrow passageway at the very front and back of the deck. There's room for only one person to walk there comfortably. Someone leaning on the rail to watch the scenery can step to one side of that spot in either direction, and there's plenty of room. No one wants to stand where there's ample space. They all want to stand in the very center, where the space is narrowest. The topper was a lovely young woman being kissed by a hairy creep while his dog lay in the passageway. When I said, "Excuse me," and tried to get by, the creep displayed a most aggravated expression. And well he should, I guess. O, for some sweet, but effective, utterance to resolve the whole matter. Again, button it up!

Carpoolian Jack Kennedy zinged me with an argument that rubbed me the wrong way. I thought about it during my ferry walk and gave him my well-thought-out perfect comeback, thinking it would stir more debate.

"Thank you, Dave." That was his only reply.

Jack handled it just right.

One time some teenagers were having a long-distance spitting contest on the upper deck. The wind carried the spittle for 10-15 yards. My back was to the contest and I felt a wet projectile on the back of my neck. I whipped around. The teens pretended not to notice. What I did then, I admit, was intimidating, and I don't recommend it, but I simply and calmly followed the young man all over the ferry, saying not a word. Finally, overcome with guilt, he apologized, offering me his hand. I shook it and vocalized my forgiveness.

My dog never says anything and triumphs in every battle of wits.

Secure, having all the self-esteem He needed, Jesus felt no need to win every argument.

And neither, I suppose, should I.

Overwhelmed with Eyewash

Suzanne becomes concerned when her daycare center must undergo relicensing. The center she manages has perhaps the best reputation in Bremerton. But it sometimes appears as though inspectors get paid by the number of discrepancies they find. "Experts" in the state capital keep dreaming up more silly rules—such as keeping the kids' nap pads so many inches apart to prevent disease. In doesn't occur to them that kids may be coughing or drooling on one another throughout the day. But keep them apart at nap time.

I told her she could ace the inspection by doing what Mr. Kozlowski did at Castle Air Force Base. He was recreation program director and had a few miles—and inspections under his belt. Any activity that ever graced the recreational facility, and every favorable note or letter he ever enticed participants to write, he proudly displayed in a thick scrapbook. When the inspector showed up, Mr. Kozlowski occupied every moment of the inspector's schedule regaling him with the glories depicted in that hefty book

Mr. Kozlowski always garnered recognition and praise at the inspector's out-brief to the Commander.

If Suzanne wants to pass those inspections, she needs to follow Mr. K's unquestioned shining example. A scrapbook can easily and readily show 'em that hers surpasses every childcare center known to humankind.

I know it is. I'm being very objective here. Parents know it's the best. The kids know. It's only fair that the inspector knows as well.

A gold-color-etched simulated leather vinyl cover is a nice touch.

Works every time.

Double Death of Divorce

How do I write about two failed marriages? My parents and extended family gave me a rich heritage of durable marriages and the faith and faithfulness that found divorce unconscionable. I never chose divorce, but I was forced to deal with it. My conscience is clear. But too often I hear about the "innocent" or "injured" spouse, and it would be too easy to say I was all of those. I cannot rightfully say, however, that in my misery I didn't contribute to theirs. Dad may have thought my double plight was part of the recurring wreckage of wars, in this case, the Vietnam era. Part of my problem was insecurity that bred, I see in retrospect, self-centeredness on my part. I remained loyal as long as they would have me. And when they no longer wanted me around, I was deeply hurt and confused.

I cannot paint my ex-spouses with the same brush. My self-centeredness prompted one or the other to see the world through a distorted window and retaliate by, perhaps, separating me from money and goods or fabricating stories. Or narrowly missing my head with a flower pot. Both picked the same unmentionable nickname for me in the end. Let's see...perhaps a quip will describe it: "They said I was Number One, but they treated me like Number Two!"

One of them asked me to take her away from her unhappy past and dreamed of happily ever after. The other was a perfectionist and thought that one who believed in a perfect God would somehow behave likewise and rescue her from her unhappy imperfections and faint hope for an untarnished world.

In both cases I should have looked beyond the charm and seen trouble brewing—unrealistic expectations in both marriages, mixed faiths in one marriage and an ill-fated rebound in the other. I sought counseling near the end of both. The first counselor, a godless man, insulted my values by saying the key to restoring my marriage was to date other women. I refused. The two positive lessons I took away from him, however, were rational thinking—don't blame one's problems on childhood or the past, but make sound decisions based on what one faces today; and I should make my decisions based on what I thought was right, and not necessarily on the dictates of others. Good! With that assurance, I fired him.

With my second marriage failing, I again sought counsel. Dr. Goldsmith was a Christian, and he had better discernment. "What's wrong with me, Doc? Why can't I succeed in marriage?" After a few sessions, he answered. "There's nothing wrong with you, Dave," he said, "except that you're a poor picker."

In my first marriage I spent far too much time selfishly glued to the TV or standing around at the audio club recording tapes. Divorce was no answer. A swift kick in the pants and some relationship skills from an authoritative or trusted person might have helped. But the real cause of selfishness to whatever degree is rebellion. I tried the "fire-insurance" coverage of my faith and that left self too much in control. D. James Kennedy nailed the problem: There are really only two kinds of faith or worship in the world: submitting to and honoring one God, as demonstrated by the Judeo-Christian tradition; or you can lump everything else—secular humanism, atheism, agnosticism, "New Age," Eastern thought—into the alternative faith: faith in self, or self-worship. Self-worship is kicking God off the throne of my heart and I pick and choose or create the rules. I might think my compassionate good deeds get me off the hook, but if they're done on my terms, and not God's, I'm still into self-worship.

I hate to admit it, but that's what led to my double-death by divorce. I reserved too much of life to my own whims and misguided wisdom, and put God in the back seat, when I'd let Him in at all. Without divine power in my life, I asked for His help when it was too late. The second time around, I made course corrections and tried to reform, but I failed again. Rather than reform, God wanted to transform. Twice defeated, I finally gave up. I surrendered. That's when He sent my soul mate into my life.

Perfection. I haven't achieved that. One wife was at best a spiritual baby. My "reformed" life did little to inspire growth. She sought perfection, and a misunderstanding of Nazarene theology further disillusioned her. She had heard of "entire sanctification" and being "perfect" as God was perfect. She sought what she thought would enable her to live without error or disappointment. But disappointed she was—in the imperfections of both herself and me. She could not bring herself to give up her hope that somehow she could achieve flawless living free of human struggles and mistakes. If only she—if only I—might have more fully understood and if I had demonstrated that spiritual perfection can be accepted as a gift from God, even if our humanity continues, defects and all, throughout life, ever growing toward that critical freedom from the enthronement of self.

Finally, I must say that both former wives are worthy human beings, created and loved by God. I hold no ill will toward them, and I pray for them often, as I do for my children and grandchildren. One is the mother of my dear children, and I pray that the other, wherever she is, has found the godly light needed to free her of her perfectionist misery and introduce her to here-and-now rest in the Lord.

Blessed now for more than a quarter century with the girl of my dreams, Suzanne, whom God so painstakingly designed for my needs, and I for hers, I can't help but think of the story of Job. Once thinking I was doomed to suffer lifelong loss and loneliness I, like Job, was restored with great joy.

After Job had prayed for his friends, the LORD made him prosperous again and gave him twice as much as he had before. All his brothers and sisters and everyone who had known him before came and ate with him in his house. They comforted and con-soled him over all the trouble the LORD had brought upon him…The LORD blessed the latter part of Job's life more than the first.

Pearl of Great Price

As I was writing my book, King's High School classmate Joyce Harrison Shaw put me onto one of the two most profound books I—or anyone—has ever read: *Divine Conspiracy*, by Dallas Willard. It dawned on me that all I was trying to say and portray in my book was so eloquently explained in his.

"We try to 'manage' or control those closest to us by blaming and condemning them and by forcing upon them our 'wonderful solutions' for their problems," Willard enlightens us. "[God] then shows us a truly effective and gracious way of caring for and helping the people we live....It is the way of the *request*, of asking."

Willard demonstrates the proven results of non-condemning living, having lived with his brother and family who lived totally without anger, manipulation, put-downs, paybacks, contempt, condemnation or forcing "pearls" upon people for whom such counsel was not welcome nor helpful.

This, he shows us in such simple terms, is the essence of the Sermon of the Mount. Most, if not all of us flawed human beings, are ill-equipped to "straighten people out."

"Parents are seen to treat their children with 'an incivility which, offered to any other young people, would simply have terminated the acquaintance.'"

O my. That's it! He has found the elusive key to the locket.

"The result of condemning and blaming is sure to be a counterattack....The parents who have reproached a child for using drugs, for example, soon find themselves condemned for coffee, tobacco, or alcohol use," Willard says. "If our counterattack is unacceptable...it may be shoved beneath the surface and will then come out in many forms of behavior that look like something else, for example, perfectionism, procrastination, rejection of authority, or passive/aggressive tendencies such as chronic tardiness or the constant aborting of success—or even in physical symptoms."

Bingo!

This reciprocity explains why condemnation as a strategy for correcting or "helping" those near and dear to us, he says, will almost always fail.

This is heady stuff.

He suggests, quite accurately, that such attacks and counterattacks birthed the generation gap, virtually unknown before the sixties.

"Popular arts, sexual morality or immorality, disenchantment with 'the establishment.' the Vietnam War and the draft, racial segregation, the role of education in society, and other factors, were all a part of the mix."

The cure, Willard points out, is an ancient one, only now being rediscovered by too few: the power of the request—both of our fellow human beings and of God.

> Do you doubt the dynamic influence of the request? The power of asking is so great that it makes many people uncomfortable. Don't you know of people who will go considerably out of their way to avoid someone who is apt to ask them for something? It may even be someone whom they do not know and will never meet again. But they do not wish to feel the power of the request. Who really enjoys eating a sandwich in front of the family dog?
>
> No matter that it is your favorite sandwich, which you have lovingly prepared as part of a tiny vacation with your book in a quiet and pleasant place, here is the face, the eyes, perhaps a paw on your knee. You know the rest. You are up against a fundamental force of the universe.

As I've said, if you read no other book, read Willard's (and his source text). Spare no effort or expense. It truly unlocks the secrets of the ages.

Good Ventriloquists and Bad

Sister Kathy gave us belly laughs when she would mimic a story-telling ventriloquist young woman who used her "talent" to earn her way through college. To see and hear Kathy's rendition, the storyteller would plaster on a Cheshire smile and attempt to speak without moving her lips. If Kathy's portrayal was accurate, the young lady wasn't very good at it. It sounded like this: "Hi, there. I'n jest so haffy to use ny talent that has din githen knee in this way to dring stories to the doys and girls!"

Then she sings,

> We are haffy feofle, fraise the Lord;
> For we have the Didle, God's own Word.
> Satan had a hold on knee
> Jesus cane and set knee free
> On the cross of Calvary
> Oh fraise the Lord.

As a late-night comedian would say of guys talking, "That's nuthin'. Listen to this!" The greatest ventriloquist I've ever seen was Kenny Woods. Jinny Woods started bringing Kenny to Fall Creek Church of the Nazarene, where I played the organ and they'd ask me to speak now and then. It was I who learned a lesson I'll never forget.

It was customary to ask someone in the congregation to open a session in prayer. I didn't know Kenny very well, but he seemed to be a friendly fellow and Jinny often contributed to the discussions. As we started, I said, "Kenny, would you please lead us in prayer?" Suddenly, he performed his ventriloquist magic. All I heard was Jinny vocalizing the prayer. And a good one it was. Kenny, a bit on the shy side, had nudged his wife who recited the prayer as if she had practiced for weeks. Eloquent.

Try as I did to choose more carefully in the future, it wasn't the last time I heard ventriloquists in similar circumstances. Wow! If I ask someone these days, I'm careful to pick someone who I know has actual conversations with the Hearer.

Don't get me wrong. Some folks talk to God incessantly, but they feel uneasy praying in public. That's OK.

Nothing worse, I guess, than calling on folks to talk publicly to a God with Whom they're not on speaking terms at all—Someone they don't know and from Whom they would just as soon spend an eternity apart. God's a gentleman. He lets them choose their own destiny. As Dallas Willard says, the fires of heaven will be hotter than those of hell. One would not choose to go to a place where heavenly choirs would just make one feel uncomfortable, working up a sweat, burning up as I've felt a couple of times standing out of place as a stranger on a stage or before a television camera, unprepared and wishing I were somewhere else. No one like that in heaven.

Sometimes I've avoided the well-lit place where I should have gone. I chose, at those times, to cower, tormented and miserable in a darkened venue, rather than having made the right choice. I felt like the ventriloquist's dummy.

I'm sure that's how eternity will be. It's a choice, and I'm hanging around the folks I want to spend it with, learning the tunes and the uplifting lyrics. Where I end up, I want to be perfectly comfortable, so I'm practicing to be prepared. Sometimes stumbling, I want to get to that point where I can't wait to go gladly and to go boldly before the throne of grace, as scripture invites us—as I've recited before: *I wanna get so close to Him that it's no big change on that day that Jesus calls my name!*

Eight Reasons Why You Might Choose Not to Go to Heaven

1. A loving God wouldn't send people to hell.

People harbor this misconception when they don't know God and have no idea what hell is all about. God is both loving and just. What would be just about inviting Hitler to spend eternity with Mother Teresa? And hell isn't necessarily literal fire. As Dallas Willard says in *The Divine Conspiracy*, "Those who do not now enter the eternal life of God though confidence in Jesus will experience separation, isolation, and the end of their hopes. Perhaps this will be permitted in their case because they have chosen to be God themselves, to be their own ultimate point of reference. God permits it, but that posture obviously can only be sustained at a distance from God.... Still, there is room in the universe for them."

If you, for example, chose to go to a place of utter separation from God, it is because you have chosen to exclude God all along life's path, by your everyday activities and preferences. You would have decided as your own god to pick and choose what you would embrace and discard from God's revealed Word. Unless you accept it all (and there are solid reasons for doing so—despite what you may have perceived in a shallow assessment) you cling to your own claim of self-deification. God has no room for other gods. You choose separation—throughout a conscious eternity—but, in realizing what you gave up, you would spend eternity in immensely sorrowful regret. Wow! Why would you do that? That's not for me!

2. I'm a good person, deserving of heaven.

God says there is none righteous; no, not one. By selective compliance—or worse yet, setting up your own set of ethics or rules instead of bonding with God in an intimate relationship (His one desire), you'd fall short. *All have sinned and come short of the glory of God,* He says. *God made him who had no sin to be sin for us, so that in him we might become the righteousness of God.* Christ's death was sufficient for the sins of the whole world, but just as you must accept a gift from your friend before it means anything, Christ's sufficiency won't do you any good until you receive Him and submit to His makeover of your life: *But to as many as did receive and welcome Him, He gave the authority (power, privilege, right) to become the children of God, that is, to those who believe in (adhere to, trust in, and rely on) His name.* (AMP)

3. I'm not good enough for God to accept me. I'll seek God if I ever clean up my act.

You will be unable to clean up your life without His work in your life, and that won't happen until you come to Him just as you are. *While we were yet in weakness [powerless to help ourselves], at the fitting time Christ died for (in behalf of) the ungodly.* (AMP) No matter how terrible your sin is (yes, it's awful—as bad as mine!), God, through his Son Jesus, eagerly looks forward to forgiving you and adopting you as his child. Nothing would delight Him more!

4. I can't accept a God who condemns people in non-Western lands who don't know any better.

Again, your concept of God is too small. Read the first chapter of Romans. Since God is just, He will not condemn an innocent person. He has a way to reach everyone. Chuck Colson in *How Now Shall We Live* writes about a girl in the atheist Soviet Union who found Christ through classical novels. Another found Him in a "still, small voice" she perceived within her. Ah! God has a way, and so Jesus can lovingly say, *I am the Way and the Truth and the Life; no one comes to the Father except by (through) Me.* (AMP) Christian Ravi Zacharias, a former Hindu priest from India, points out that Christless religions are exclusionary, despite the perceptions of many. But Christ, our loving and living advocate, is "not willing that any should perish," providing the gift of redemption to all who will receive it, and He has provided abundant archaeological, historical, scientific and prophetic evidence that He is who He claims to be.

5. I see too much hypocrisy, Inquisitions and bloody Crusades to believe in Christ.

Are these violations of Christ's teachings or demonstrations of them? The more you focus on Christ, the more you see the treasure and less the vessel.

6. I cannot accept a God who allows so much suffering in the world.

Suffering was unknown in Eden. Sin brought suffering into the world. Lee Strobel, in *A Case for Faith*, tells of a man who ran over his toddler in the driveway. "So deep was Marc's initial despair that he had to ask God to help him breathe, to help him eat…. Otherwise he was paralyzed by the emotional pain. But he increasingly felt God's presence, his grace, his warmth, his comfort, and very slowly, over time, his wounds began to heal." He was able to help others as a result of his pain. "Now other hearts were being healed because of Marc's having been broken." The answer to pain and suffering is the presence of Jesus himself. John R. W. Stott, cited by Strobel, says, "I could never myself believe in God, if it were not for the cross…. In the real world of pain, how could one worship a God who was immune to it…. In imagination I have turned…to that lonely, twisted, tortured figure on the cross, nails through hands and feet, back lacerated, limbs wrenched, brow bleeding from thorn-pricks, mouth dry and intolerably thirsty, plunged in God-forsaken darkness. That is the God for me! He laid aside his immunity to pain. He entered our world of flesh and blood, tears and death. He suffered for us. Our sufferings become more manageable in light of his." Strobel asks, "How have difficulties, challenges and even pain shaped your character and values?" He concludes with insight from Peter Kreeft, "I believe all suffering contains at least the opportunity for good."

7. I'm having too much fun without God.

My associate Jim Helsley thought that way. Learning he had terminal bone cancer he went out and bought a new Jaguar. He was going to enjoy life and face death without trusting God. Darwin's theories, now largely discredited in acknowledgement by scientists of an intelligent designer, resulted in people being taught that they are an accident of nature, leading lives without meaning. God alone can provide genuine meaning to your life, and only with a meaningful life can one experience true, lasting pleasure. I'm having too much fun *with* God. My life would be miserable without Him, lacking purpose. I cannot imagine such a life. My heart grieves for those who dismiss Him. Scripture teaches three reasons to turn your back on Him: ignorance, pride and/or a moral problem. I've found this to be true in every conversation I have had with a non-believer. Believers I know have a true zest for life. Oh sure, I've found believers who aren't having much fun. Usually it's because of self-imposed bondage that has no basis in Christ's teachings, but in man-made rules—again focusing on the vessel (organization) more than the treasure.

8. Evangelical Christians I've seen aren't the brightest bulbs on the tree. "They are largely poor, uneducated and easy to command."—*Washington Post*, Feb. 1, 1993 (later recanted)

Three responses:

a. This uninformed perception comes from possible static in the transmission, coming or going. The dullard may have a garbled understanding of the spectacular offerings of the Christian life and worldview, or you may not know the person sufficiently—what are his or her strengths and weaknesses?

b. Spiritual insight is not dependent on intellect: *For the foolishness of God is wiser than man's wisdom, and the weakness of God is stronger than man's strength. Brothers, think of what you were when you were called. Not many of you were wise by human standards; not many were influential; not many were of noble birth.* I Corinthians 1: 25-26 (NIV)

c. The most brilliant people I've read or heard are Christians: Charles Colson, C.S. Lewis, D. James Kennedy, and Ravi Zacharias, among them. As Kennedy points out, the University of Paris, Oxford, Cambridge, Harvard, Yale, Dartmouth, Princeton and virtually all of the first 123 universities and colleges established in America were founded by Christians. People who believed in the Bible originated just about every branch of science. They thought of themselves as "thinking God's thoughts after him." Here are some of them: Louis Pasteur, bacteriology; Johannes Kepler, celestial mechanics; Lord Kelvin, energetics; Blaise Pascal, hydrostatics; Charles Babbage, computer science; Lord Joseph Lister, antiseptic surgery; Robert Boyle, chemistry; James Simpson, anesthesiology; Matthew Fontaine Maury, oceanography; Samuel Morse, telegraphy; and Sir Isaac Newton, calculus and dynamics.

I titled this chapter with reasons *not* to go to heaven. As inviting as going home to heaven sounds to me, it's intimacy with Jesus that holds the most benefit. Grafted with Him, here and now, generates heaven on earth. My faith is not a religion. It's a relationship. How about you? Let's talk.

Divine Appointment

I was so enthralled with Dallas Willard's book, *Divine Conspiracy*, that I volunteered to teach it for adult Sunday School. Nothing the pastor could say to promote the concepts of the book could do it justice, and I was concerned that no one would show up for my class on this incredible volume. It was a bit deep, and my objective was that our discussions would bring it down to earth.

Ethyl Zaren showed up for the class, bringing her friend and co-worker Robyn. Ethel had known the Lord for years, but she said this was her first adult Sunday School class.

She bought the book, but she seemed less interested in discussions about its contents than our sharing personal experiences from our lives. Perhaps that's what God intended. Ethel showed a picture of her grandfather as a child in a loincloth in Colombia. A missionary couple had adopted him and he returned with them to the States, where he eventually taught in a Bible school.

Ethel, 46, had had a tough life, went through a divorce and raised children to adulthood as a single mom. She now taught at a day care center on Bangor, the nearby Navy base.

Perhaps thinking they'd help populate the sparsely attended class, Suzanne, brother-in-law John and his folks, Warren and Jean, attended.

Our meeting together for 13 weeks was divinely appointed. Midway through the quarter, Ethel showed up with her three young grandchildren from California.

"My daughter is dying from cancer, and I have custody of the children," she said.

The small class rallied to this family's aid like nothing I had ever seen. The next few weeks and months were a blur, but during that time, John arranged for Ethel to purchase a mobile home, Warren and Jean willingly risked their life savings to finance the transaction, and church people stepped up with furniture, food, clothing and toys. After a few months, the daughter died, Ethel took custody of a fourth grandchild, and John made arrangements for the funeral and related substantial expenses.

That small group—perhaps no more than eight strong, five of us with family ties, listened to God's prompting on behalf of His family members who were going through a difficult time in their lives.

Ethel and her grandchildren beam when we see them, eyes lighting up. There's no more fulfilling activity than doing God's bidding.

God takes care of our business when we take care of His.

Religion that God our Father accepts as pure and faultless is this: to look after orphans and widows in their distress and to keep oneself from being polluted by the world. James 1:27 (NIV)

Effie

The first time I met Brad Schultz at the Corps of Engineers, I knew he was a brother, about my age, full of zest for life.

One day it was just he and I at our weekly Bible study. He told me of a "gift" an upper classman had given him in Officer Candidate School during the Vietnam era.

The gift had a name, "Effie," or "FE"—false enthusiasm. He learned to exude a positive spirit no matter what the circumstances, even while the enemy shot at him in Vietnam. "Gosh, it's good to be in the U.S. Army," he would say during such crises.

Despite aches and pains from an automobile accident, he always has a brisk step and runs up the stairs, while younger, healthier employees slowly shuffle to their desks.

At first, one might be troubled by the "false" nature of the practice, but Brad says ultimately it's not false at all. By practicing enthusiasm all the time, the false part fades and the positive attitude becomes genuine.

No surprise. Enthusiasm means inspired, and comes from *theos*, or God, as in "God within," or "the Spirit within." God converts the false life we once pursued—based on self—and turns it into authentic living.

I've met a few other folks who act like Brad. I recall a short Bible teacher leading a seminar who, even early in the morning, was full of energy. Students kept asking him his secret, and he kept deferring, saying he'd tell us later. After many reminders and pleadings, he relented. He hopped up on the platform and started running in place, shouting, "If you *act* enthusiastic, you will *be* enthusiastic! If you *act* enthusiastic, you will *be* enthusiastic! If you *act* enthusiastic, you will *be* enthusiastic!"

He, like Brad, had discovered the powerful energy of God within.

I hadn't told Brad that story, but he found the truth on his own.

"When I was talking to Effie, I discovered I had really been talking to the Holy Spirit all along."

Parallel Lives

I wonder if someone parallels everyone else's life as Don Johnson paralleled mine—or vice versa. Don was frugal in his first marriage. So was I. He'd drive the length of town to get the best gas prices. He lived in Minneapolis and moved to Seattle. Same here. He worked for the Army Corps of Engineers in Seattle. Me, too.

He had work assignments in Japan, Korea, Germany and Saudi Arabia. Just like me. He associated with missionaries overseas. As did I. One of them baptized me in Korea. There, I met up with Don and expressed concern that Vice President Spiro Agnew had announced that our Air Force F-4 Phantom fighter wing would move to Korea from Misawa Air Base, Japan, my previous assignment. In so doing, the bottom dropped out of the housing market at Misawa. Eighteen months earlier I thought I closed the best housing purchase in history—a three-bedroom carpeted and tatami-matted home for my family and me. I bought it for $4,500. I had little choice but to sell it to a Japanese family for $1,500 before reporting to my new assignment alone in Korea. In fact, the staffer on base recording the purchases said my sale price was the highest he'd seen after Agnew's announcement in 1970. Some new homes, originally bought by airmen for nearly twice what I paid, sold for $500…$50…and some bills of sale indicated a title transfer for a sale price of $0.

Don listened to my story and assured me I had no problem. The Homeowners' Assistance Act would pick up the tab for service members under such circumstances. He said the Corps of Engineers administered the program. He'd check into my situation. Sure enough, about a month later a check arrived in the mail from the Corps made payable to me in the amount of $3,019—more than enough to make up the difference.

Don remarried after his first wife died. I remarried, too, after the death of divorce. He enjoyed the benefit of retiring from the Air Force Reserve as a lieutenant colonel. What a coincidence! Likewise.

Lt. Col. Don Johnson, USAFR, retired, suffered a heart attack and met an untimely demise…

Cut!

I trust that's where the parallel ends. Let's not get ridiculous about this and carry it to extremes!

...and Lt. Col. Dave Harris, USAFR, retired, lived happily ever after.

For further reading, with great pleasure I recommend the following:

Greg Asimakoupoulos, *Draw Me Close to You* (Nashville, Integrity Publishers, 2003)

Charles Colson and Nancy Pearcey, *How Now Shall We Live?* (Wheaton: Tyndale House Publishers, 1999)

Lee Strobel, *The Case for Faith* (Grand Rapids: Zondervan Publishing House, 2000)

Dallas Willard, *Divine Conspiracy* (New York: HarperCollins Publishers, 1998)

Ravi Zacharias, *Can Man Live Without God* (Dallas: Word Publishing, 1994)

E-mail me at **davegharris@earthlink.net**

0-595-31311-6

Printed in the United States
22472LVS00003B/190-213

9 780595 313112